Praise Through

Poetry . . .

Prayers . . .

And Prose

Second Edition

By: Leigh

All scripture quotations are from the King James Version of
the Bible unless otherwise noted.
Scripture labeled NIV is from the New International Version
of the Bible, Published by Tyndale House Publishers, Inc
Wheaton, IL
And
Zondervan
Grand Rapids MI

Scripture labeled NKJV is from the New King James Version
of the Bible Publisher by
Thomas Nelson Publishers, Inc
Nashville. Camden. New York

"Thou shalt not muzzle the ox that treadeth out the corn. And
the labourer is worthy of his reward." I Tim 5:18 (I Cor 9:9,
Deut 24:15

"Therefore, behold, I am against the prophets, saith the Lord,
that steal my words every one from his neighbor." Jer 23:30
"…Thou shalt not steal, … Thou shalt love thy neighbor as
thyself." Rom 13:9, (Matt 19:18, Mark 10:19, Luke 18:20, I
Cor 6:8,10, Eph 4:28, ex 20:15, Lev 19:11, 13, 18, Matt 5:43,
7:12, 19:19, 22:39, Mark 12:31, Gal 5:14, James 2:8)

" Render therefore to all their dues: … honor to whom honor."
Rom 13:7 "That no man go beyond and defraud his brother in
any matter: because that the lord is the avenger of all such, as
we also have forwarded you and testified." I Thes 4:6 (Lev
19:13, Deut 32:35, Proverbs 22:22,23) Scriptures complied by the
Bluedorns, Triviumpursuit.com

ISBN: 978-0-9794612-5-5

Praise Through Poetry, Prayers and Prose
Second Edition

Dedication:

God is the 'giver of all good gifts.' He alone gave me the Poetry, Prayers, Prose and Insights enclosed herein. And so, once again I give His gifts back to Him while sharing them with you, too! Thank You, Jesus!

Psalms 121:

"I will lift up mine eyes unto the hills, from
whence cometh my help. My help cometh
from the LORD, which made heaven and earth.
HE will not suffer my foot to be moved: He that
keepeth thee (me) will not slumber. Behold, HE
that keepeth Israel shall neither slumber nor sleep.
The LORD is thy (my) keeper: the LORD is thy
(my) shade upon my right hand. The sun shall not
smite thee (me) by day, nor the moon by night.
The Lord shall preserve thee (me) from all evil:
He shall preserve thy (my) soul. The LORD shall
preserve thy (my) going out and thy (my) coming
in from this time forth and even for evermore."

~*~

And so I choose to praise HIM with my whole
being. The "fruit of my lips giving thanks"
unto my GOD and KING JESUS, Amen!

~*~

Thus the reason for this second edition.

GOD

As Father ...

Creator ...

Savior ...

Etc.

God's Smile!

God's Loving Hands

God's loving hands
Feel the warmth within the Father's touch
God's loving hands
Feel the Love He wants to share so much
He's reaching out
to touch your darkened life today
He'll bring it Light
and you can live a whole new way
God's loving hands
Feel the Peace within the Father's touch
Won't you reach out
He wants to hold you very much
And as you grow
He'll bring new victories everyday
He'll hold you up
And guide you all along life's way
God's loving hands
Will teach you Love and Joy divine
As long as your grip
On Him is firm all will be fine
No matter how rough
The trail appears in front of you
He'll ALWAYS be there
To see that you will make it through
God's loving hands
Feel the warmth within the Father's touch
God's loving hands
Feel the Love He wants to share so much
He Loves us so He sacrificed His only Son
He did it for you as if you were the only one

God's loving hands
Feel HIS Love
HIS is the REAL One!

God's Redeeming Love

Redeeming Love, so simple and true
'Tis why our Lord died for me and you
Before your life was e're foretold
He gave His in an act so bold
To save mankind from their sin
And begin His reign inside of them
He walked the road right through town
All the while wearing that thorny crown
Beaten, Scourged and spat upon
Yet like a lamb He remained dumb
Nailed upon a lowly tree
There on that hill for all to see
He gave His life for you and me
And as He took His final breath
He surrendered His Spirit unto death
"It is finished," He did say
And the temple veil split in two that day
There is no more dividing wall
His Love is free to one and all
But this was not His end, you see
Just the beginning for you and me
For three days later He rose from the
tomb
Relieving sorrow and lifting gloom
As He met His friends in the upper room
This resurrection life, you see
Is what He gives to you and me
When we leave our sins upon His cross
And count our lives as but a loss
His Spirit comes to dwell within
And thus we become "born again"
Redeeming Love, it cost so much
Yet is freely given by His simple touch
Accept this loving gift from Him
Be freed from sin
Let His Spirit in!

Daddy - God

Your word calls You the Everlasting
Father. Yet in my darkest moments,
When I am alone and afraid, I want my
Daddy near. To sit on Your lap and feel
The protective strength in Your loving
Arms as they wrap around me and hold
Me close. Even though I may age in this
Physical body, I will always be Your
Child. And when my way seems rough,
Twisted and bumpy, I know that at the
End of the day, or when I am at my
Weakest, I can crawl up into that
Protective place in your lap and cry.
My Daddy, my God, will heal all of my
Hurts.
Thanks, Daddy!

~*~

For you have not received a spirit of
Bondage again to fear, but ye have
Received the Spirit of adoption, whereby
We cry, Abba (Daddy), Father.
Romans 8:15

Daddy

I listen to hear Your voice, waiting patiently.
I speak and the outpouring of my lips is Your Words
Giving comfort and direction to all those I meet.

I walk and it is Your path my feet trod,
Leading me right to Your throne of grace.
I sit in Your lap and find shelter from the
cares of this life, rest for my weary bones
and a sweet smile on Your face.
And Your smile lightens my load.

As I wait I am refreshed body, soul and spirit.
And when You speak to me in that moment,
You say: "Well done My child"
And all is well in the world!

~*~

"Let the words of my mouth, and the
meditation of my heart, be acceptable in
Thy sight, O Lord, my strength and my
Redeemer." Psalms 19:14 KJV

God Owns All Of Creation

God owns all of creation
He made it all and gave it life.
Yet we turn our backs to live in strife.
He gave us life with that first breath.
And once again when He chose His own death.

He bought us back from the enemy
To give us a home for eternity.
But with the choices that we make
We tell Him His plan's not so great.

We choose to follow a lie instead
Of following Jesus where He has led.
And yet He stands with His arms out wide
Continually drawing us back to His side.

"Repent," He says, "and live anew.
And I will give you freedom, too."
O're sin, hell, death and the grave
He alone has the power to save.

Give back to Him what is truly His
And learn what it is to REALLY live!

~*~

"The earth is the Lord's, and everything in it.
The world and all it's people belong to Him"
Psalms 24:1

The Potter

Yes Lord, I'm but a Lump of clay
Spinning on the Wheel
Mold me in just the right way
As I'm yielded to Your will

Change me to that perfect shape
That I, Your vessel may be
Used to pour forth Your Holy Spirit
That others may drink of Thee

~*~

"Does not the Potter have the right to
Make out of the same lump of clay some
Pottery for noble purposes and some for
Common use?" Romans 9:21 NIV

JEHOVAH

Jesus

Everlasting Father

Holy One

Only Begotten of the Father

Victorious Over Death, Hell and the grave

Almighty God

Happy to Bless HIS People

~*~

"That men may know that thou, whose name
Alone is Jehovah, art the Most High over all
The earth." Psalms 83:18

Jesus Is Our Light

Jesus is our Light,
As we walk this dark earth
May we in Him shine bright,
And show forth His wondrous worth

To a world in darkness lost
knowing not which way to go
Who Satan has bitterly tossed about
Who are wandering aimless, to and fro

As we shine forth in His Light
Guiding others in and to the Way
May we reflect His Light and Love
More clearly day by day

~*~

The night is far spent, the day is at hand:
therefore cast off the works of darkness,
and let us put on the armor of Light
Romans 13:1

The Way, The Truth, and The Life

You are the Way
Along life's path
And I shall follow Thee

You are the Truth
And by Your Word
From sin I am set free

You are the Life
And by Your power
I'll live abundantly

And I shall live on heaven's shores
With Thee eternally!

~*~

… I am going there to prepare a place for you. And if I go and prepare a place for you, I will come back and take you to be with me that you also may be where I am. You know the way to the place where I am going." Thomas said to him, "Lord, we don't know where you are going, so how can we know the way?" Jesus answered, "I am the way and the truth and the life. No one comes to the Father except through me. John 14:2b-6 NIV

LIGHT

Light in the darkness
You are to the world.
Dispelling the mists
And enlightening the soul

Igniting a flame
That burns from within
And beams from the eyes
Illuminating the whole

Glowing supremely
As we pass it along
In a word, a prayer,
Or even a song

Heavenly healing
Flows through the bones
And sin is erased
As Jesus sits on the throne

Thus it is written
In the Bible we read:
"I am the Light of the world."
"Come follow Me!"

Then spake Jesus again unto them, saying, I am the light of the world:
he that followeth me shall not walk in darkness, but shall have the
light of life. John 8:12 KJV
…Ye are the light of the world. A city that is set on an hill cannot be
hid. Neither do men light a candle, and put it under a bushel, but on a

candlestick; and it giveth light unto all that are in the house. Let your light so shine before men, that they may see your good works, and glorify your Father which is in heaven. Matthew 5:14-16 KJV

The Cross In The Center

The Cross In The Center

There in the center Christ died
Our forgiveness to provide

Acceptance was on His right side
A thief gave up his foolish pride
He now walks with Jesus
And there to forever abide

Rejection was there on His left
Angry and mocking at his death
Another man rightly convicted of theft
Was attacking Jesus with his final breaths

He recognized not the King
Who was dying his freedom to bring
He died alone in his sin and shame
And he only had himself to blame

Today as you look at Calvary's tree
Tell me, on which side will you be?

~*~

Then were there two thieves crucified with him, one on the right hand, and another on the left And when they were come to the place, which is called Calvary, there they crucified him, and the malefactors, one on the right hand, and the other on the left ... And one of the malefactors which were hanged railed on him, saying, If thou be Christ, save thyself and us. But the other answering rebuked him, saying, dost not thou fear God, seeing thou art in the same condemnation? And we indeed justly; for we receive the due reward of our deeds: but this man hath done nothing amiss. And he said unto Jesus, Lord, remember me when thou comest into thy kingdom. And Jesus said unto him, Verily I say unto thee, today shalt thou be with me in paradise. Luke 23:32, 39-43 KJV

The Resurrection

Before sunrise in the Garden
Jesus in the tomb was still hid
How will they find Him?
Who'll remove the tomb's lid?

The guards have all been scattered
They are scared quite to death
While telling the officials their story
They are all out of breath

Morning has now broken
But the sky is dark and gray
The women have all gathered
Homage and respect to pay

The ground has been shaken
The stone's been rolled away
The body of Christ has disappeared
Where has it been laid?

Their Lord and Master's missing
The women are confused
The wrappings are laying there
All tangled up and used

Over on the bench
The face cloth solemnly lays
Neatly folded like a napkin
I will return, it says

The women leave the Garden
Weeping as they go
A man in white stands near by
Oh sir, where is our Lord?

It is I, He gently whispers
Why are you so sad?
I've conquered death as I promised
Tis time now to be glad.

Go tell my disciples
In Jerusalem we'll meet
Return to the upper room
Where supper last we did eat.

I will join you up there
Make sure Peter knows to come
I have some last instructions
Before I leave for home

Mary had stayed in the Garden
When the other women left
She wandered off through the pathways
She was feeling so bereft

There she saw the Savior
But thought the gardener was He
Where have they laid my Master?
Please sir, tell me where can He be?

Oh Mary, don't you know Me?
Have you forgotten My very face?
Don't you remember My words of kindness?
Do you not yet feel My last embrace?

Oh, Lord, you're alive
Really standing next to me
I thought the ruling elders
Had done away with Thee

Mary, I have risen
Conquered death, hell and the grave
I have complete the Father's work
Lost souls can now be saved.

But Mary, please don't touch me
I have not My Father seen
But run now to My disciples
Tell them with you I have been

So Mary met the disciples
All gathered in the room
They had locked themselves inside it
And were all filled with such gloom

Peter was dejected
He was not within the fold
His Lord he had rejected
When hours before he'd been so bold

Peter came into the meeting
But he stayed off to the side
He shouldn't be here greeting
The One whose life he'd just denied

Jesus came into the building
Without opening the lock
The disciples were all humbled
And Peter was in shock

Jesus stood before those gathered
All their fears He did calm
He proved He was not a ghost
As showed His feet, side and palms

When the crowd believed He was risen
He left and went his way
He walked the road to Emmaus
With other disciples did He stay

He taught them from the lessons
He had shared throughout the years
And when He blessed and broke the bread
Shortly after He disappeared

This got the men to thinking
Of all the lessons He did teach
So in the dark they left the house
Jerusalem they had to reach

Arriving in the city
Of David their earlier king
They went into the upper room
The news of Jesus they did sing

And each one had a story
Of how they'd seen the Lord
How He'd shown Himself unto them
And gave them all a new word

Resurrection he had called it
For He had raised to life again
And when in time He comes for us
We will our Resurrection win

We will truly be like Jesus
Death and sin will be erased
On that day we'll live forever
When we see Him face to Face!

GIFT

Going against the grain

Interaction and **I**nvitation

Faithfulness of the **F**ather

Treasure too abundant to measure

Jesus <u>is</u> our GIFT!

~*~

For God so loved the world that He <u>GAVE</u> His only begotten Son, that whosoever believeth on Him should not perish, but have everlasting life. John 3:16

At The Cross

'Tis mercy at the cross for me
Mercy full, rich and free
Dying there on Calvary
'Tis mercy that He gave to me

'Tis Love there at the cross for me
His life He gave unselfishly
Pouring out His Love unendingly
'Tis His Love poured forth from Calvary

'Tis Forgiveness at the cross for me
For as He died in agony
He said; "Father forgive them"
'Tis forgiveness He spoke for you and me

Thank You, my Lord,
For the cross at Calvary!

~*~

But God forbid that I should glory, save in the cross of our Lord Jesus
Christ, by whom the world is crucified unto me, and I unto the world.
Galatians 6:14

Lord of All Creation

Lord, You spoke and the earth was. With
A wave of Your outstretched arm You put
The stars in their places. You formed the
Dust of the earth and breathed life into it
And man was "born."

Who are we, these beings of dust and dirt,
That You should even take notice of us?
And yet, everything You've done since the
Very beginning of time was done to draw
Us unto Your side in a loving and faithful
Relationship of Worship and Great Grace.

Thank You, Lord!

~*~

And now, finally, GOD answered Job from the eye of a violent storm.
He said: "Why do you confuse the issue? Why do you talk without
knowing what you're talking about? Pull yourself together, Job! Up
on your feet! Stand tall! I have some questions for you, and I want
some straight answers. Where were you when I created the earth?
Tell me, since you know so much! Who decided on its size? Certainly
you'll know that!
Job 38: 1-4 The Message Bible

Jesus, Our Rock

Rocks come in many sizes and shapes. There is the boulder we hide behind for safety and protection in the battle.

- Bow down thine ear to me; deliver me speedily: be thou my strong rock, for an house of defense to save me. For thou art my rock and my fortress; therefore for thy name's sake lead me, and guide me. Psalm 31:2-3 KJV

There is the weight which anchors a ship in a safe harbor or our soul in a place of rest from our enemy.

- Because God wanted to make the unchanging nature of his purpose very clear to the heirs of what was promised, he confirmed it with an oath. [18]God did this so that, by two unchangeable things in which it is impossible for God to lie, we who have fled to take hold of the hope offered to us may be greatly encouraged. [19]We have this hope as an anchor for the soul, firm and secure. It enters the inner sanctuary behind the curtain, [20]where Jesus, who went before us, has entered on our behalf. He has become a high priest forever, in the order of Melchizedek. Hebrews 6:17-20 NIV

And there is the rock we pelt our enemy with when he is chasing us through the fields of torment.

- And he [David] took his staff in his hand, and chose him five smooth stones out of the brook, and put them in a shepherd's bag which he had, even in a scrip; and his sling was in his hand: and he drew near to the Philistine ... And it came to pass, when the Philistine arose, and came, and drew nigh to meet David, that David hastened, and ran toward the army to meet the Philistine. And David put his hand in his bag, and took thence a stone, and slang it, and smote the Philistine in his forehead, that the stone sunk into his forehead; and he fell upon his face to the earth. I Samuel 17:40, 48-49 KJV

There is also the split (or cleft) in the canyon wall where we can hide to wait out the storms of life and we can surely see His glory while we are hidden there.

- And it shall come to pass, while my glory passeth by, that I will put thee in a cleft of the rock, and will cover thee with my hand while I pass by. Exodus 33:22

Jesus is all of these and so much more in our times of need!

~*~

And did all drink the same spiritual drink: for they drank of that spiritual Rock that followed them: and that Rock was Christ.
I Corinthians 10:4

S A V I O R

Son of God
And of man
Victorious over death and sin
Immanuel, God with us is He
Our faithful Father and
Righteous King!

~*~

I, even I, am the LORD; and beside me there Is no savior. I have declared, and have saved, And I have shewed, when there was no strange God among you: therefore ye are my witnesses, Saith the LORD, that I am God.
Isaiah 43:11, 12

~*~

Now to Him that is able to keep you from falling, and present you faultless before the presence of His glory with exceeding
Joy, to the only wise God our Savior, be glory and majesty, dominion and power, both now and forever. Amen. Jude 24 & 25

Jesus For the Defense

Jesus is our advocate
Who stands in front of thee
When before the Righteous Judge
We appear, so humbly
Satan, too, is present
With his lying, mocking throng
But Jesus says, 'Be still and know the
Salvation of your God.'

When Satan and his evil ones
have finished casting blame
Jesus says, 'All is forgiven,
I bore it with my shame.'
No defense lawyer on earth below
Could speak as eloquent
As the simple act of love Christ spoke,
When to the cross He went

And as His life blood ebbed away
He spoke to the Lord above
Though His words weren't eloquent
They were filled with everlasting love
'Father, God forgive them,
For they know not what they do.'
He spoke; not just for those present,
But also for me and you!

Thank You, Jesus!

~*~

But let all those that put their trust in Thee rejoice: let them shout for joy, because thou defendest them: let them also that love thy name be joyful in thee. Psalm 5:11

~*~

My little children, these things write I unto you, that ye sin not. And if any man sin, we have an advocate with the Father, Jesus Christ the righteous: And he is the propitiation for our sins: and not for ours only, but also for the sins of the whole world. And hereby we do know that we know him, If we keep his commandments. 1 John 2:1-3

MASTER

My Lord, Jesus
Almighty God
Savior
Teacher
Everlasting Father
Redeemer

And my Very Best Friend!

~*~

No man can serve two masters: for either he will hate the one, and love the other; or he will hold to the one and despise the other. Matthew 6:24

Christmas

Getting Ready for Christmas

Christmas Candy, sticky and sweet
This is what the children would like eat
But Momma's in the kitchen
The ham is in the oven
What a wonderful way she has
Of showing us her lovin'

Dad is in the back yard
Shortening the tree
So it will fit in the front room
For everyone to see

Grandma's baking cookies
Papa's in the shed
Packing out the stockings
White and green and red

Auntie's in the parlor
Stringing popcorn for the tree
Her chain would be getting longer
If it wasn't for me

We're all getting ready for Christmas
Whatever it may take
The pies are on the buffet
But where's the Birthday Cake?

You know it's Jesus' birthday
A celebration for our King
What gift will you bring Him?
What songs will you sing?

I baked a cake for Jesus
The best I ever made
I put flowers on the borders
And chocolate in the glaze

A gift I made for Jesus
And put it in a box
I wrapped it with red paper
But the ribbon was full of knots

Inside my gift was simple
A heart of paper gold
I wrote a verse upon it's back
And here my story told

I give my heart to Jesus
My Savior and my King
And though it's made of paper
It is my dearest thing

I do not have much money
To by a costly gift
But Lord, this paper heart
Is worth more that all of it

A picture of all that's in my mind
To give to You, my King
For if I could, I would give
To You my every thing!

The feast is on the table
The candle's are burning low
The family has all gathered
On each face is a glow

We're ready to celebrate Christmas
The Birthday of our King
We give thanks for all we have
And to Him our praises we sing

Happy Birthday Jesus
I'll save you a piece of cake
Thank You for the Love You gave
And that all my sins You take!

Happy Birthday Jesus
My Savior and My King
Praises I will raise to You
And ALWAYS I'll give You everything

Son of Man ~ Son of God

Born of Mary, born of God
Through the earth, like us, He trod
Battled Satan like we do
To prove He was a man, like you

Prayed the Father, "Not My will"
Before He walked up Calvary's hill
There He paid for all our sin
Victory over death to win

He showed us how this earth to trod
This Son of Man ~ This Son of God!

Thank You, Jesus!
Happy Birthday!

~*~

"But He held His peace, and answered nothing. Again the high priest
asked Him, and said unto Him, 'Art thou the Christ, the son of the
Blessed?' And Jesus I am, and ye shall see the Son of man sitting on
the right hand of power, and coming in the clouds of heaven."
Mark 14:61,62

Christmas Angels

As the angels sang
Christ was born
That very first
Christmas Morn

Let us join with them
And sing their song
And invite others
To sing along!

~*~

"And there was with the angel a multitude of heavenly host praising God, and saying; Glory to God in the highest, and on earth peace, good will toward men." Luke 2:13, 14

The Gifts We Bring

Merry Christmas to you
Is what we always hear
But do you know whose birthday
Comes this time of year?

It's the birthday of our Savior
Born to be the king
Gather 'round Him quickly
Your best gifts do bring

Not of Gold nor Silver
Nor of beads and string
But gifts of Praise and Worship
These to Him, we bring

Happy birthday, Jesus
This we gladly sing
Sharing Your gift with loved ones
While we give You everything!

~*~

And when they were come into the house, they saw the young child with Mary his mother, and fell down, and worshipped him: and when they had opened their treasures, they presented unto him gifts; *gold, and frankincense and myrrh.*
Matthew 2:11 KJV

What Is Christmas?

1. Christmas is more than just Santa and such
Santa is nice, but He isn't enough
Christmas is more than just Holly and wreaths
These may be pretty, but are so incomplete
Christmas is more than just wrappings and strings
Pretty as they are, they are still only things
Christmas is more than the presents we give
Presents are great, but they don't help us live

Chorus:
Christmas is for Jesus' birthday you see
He came down to earth just to die on a tree
He loves us all that his life he did give
He laid it down so that forever we'd live
Trust in Him and just call on His name
He'll save you from sin; He has taken your blame

2. So what is the reason for Christmas, you ask
It is the day God decide to start winning us back
He sent us His Son as a babe on the hay
Jesus came on that very first Christmas Day
Jesus was born in the town of Bethlehem
The shepherds were told and the wisemen knew when
He was born in a stable, in a manger he did lay
The Inns were all full and sent them away

Chorus:
Christmas is for Jesus' birthday you see
He came down to earth just to die on a tree
He loves us all that his life he did give
He laid it down so that forever we'd live
Trust in Him and just call on His name
He'll save you from sin; He has taken your blame

3. Angels came singing to announce Jesus birth
They told of the reason He came down to earth
They told the shepherds and then flew away
The shepherds' cam to visit the very same day
The wisemen came from the east very far
The had learned of a new King and followed His star
But no one else in the earth seemed to hear

The birth of their Savior seemed to fall on deaf ears

Chorus:
Christmas is for Jesus' birthday you see
He came down to earth just to die on a tree
He loves us all that his life he did give
He laid it down so that forever we'd live
Trust in Him and just call on His name
He'll save you from sin; He has taken your blame

4. The wisemen stopped in city of peace
But the king was not happy to see them in the least
His councilors told him of the star in the sky
He spoke to the wise men, he was being so sly
He asked the travelers again to return
He wanted the home of this new King to learn
But he was only trying to save his own neck
Soldiers killed the baby boys and homes did wreck

Chorus:
Christmas is for Jesus' birthday you see
He came down to earth just to die on a tree
He loves us all that his life he did give
He laid it down so that forever we'd live
Trust in Him and just call on His name
He'll save you from sin; He has taken your blame

5. Even as a babe men were seeking His life
Joseph hid Jesus and Mary, his wife
To Egypt they traveled and lived for a while
They lived on the gifts the wisemen gave to the Child
Joseph was told in a dream on night
The king was now dead, they could return from their flight
Joseph was scared, did he dare return home
He heard the king's son had taken the throne

Chorus:
Christmas is for Jesus' birthday you see
He came down to earth just to die on a tree
He loves us all that his life he did give
He laid it down so that forever we'd live
Trust in Him and just call on His name
He'll save you from sin; He has taken your blame

6. The family did to the town Nazareth move
Mary and Joseph returned to the place they had loved
Jesus grew up in stature and grace
He knew that one day he would be taking our place
His cousin John did prepare the way
And Jesus was baptized by him one great day
Ministering for three years all over the earth
He was telling all men that they needed new birth

Chorus:
Christmas is for Jesus' birthday you see
He came down to earth just to die on a tree
He loves us all that his life he did give
He laid it down so that forever we'd live
Trust in Him and just call on His name
He'll save you from sin; He has taken your blame

7. Jesus did the rile up the Religiously Right
So they gathered the soldiers and took Him by night
In the darkness His disciples had fled
To a kangaroo court our precious Savior was led
They questioned Him, beat Him and spat in His face
They pulled put His beard, it was such a disgrace
They sent Him to Pilate who sentenced Him to die
They lead Him to Calvary there to crucify

Chorus:
Christmas is for Jesus' birthday you see
He came down to earth just to die on a tree
He loves us all that his life he did give
He laid it down so that forever we'd live
Trust in Him and just call on His name
He'll save you from sin; He has taken your blame

8. The buried our King in a borrowed tomb
And for three days such a heaviness did loom
But the third day the earth shook, the stone rolled away
The disciples saw Jesus and there was rejoicing that day
He told them to tarry for the Spirit to fall
Then to travel the earth sharing His message to all
When He had done all He was sent to complete
He returned to heaven and took up His seat

Chorus:
Christmas is for Jesus' birthday you see
He came down to earth just to die on a tree
He loves us all that his life he did give
He laid it down so that forever we'd live
Trust in Him and just call on His name
He'll save you from sin; He has taken your blame

9. He's coming back soon, His bride to retrieve
Are you one of us? He wants no one to leave
The marriage supper we will attend with our King
There will be feasting and dancing and praises to sing
Hallelujahs will chorus thru the heavenly halls
Forever their echoes will bounce off the walls
For this is the reason that Christmas was given
God wanted all peoples with Him to be forever livin'

Chorus:
Christmas is for Jesus' birthday you see
He came down to earth just to die on a tree
He loves us all that his life he did give
He laid it down so that forever we'd live
Trust in Him and just call on His name
He'll save you from sin; He has taken your blame

Refrain:
Thank You, Jesus for coming on Christmas to give
Salvation to all so that with you we would live!
Repeat Chorus again!

Silent Night?

The nights are not so silent, But boy are they MERRY
The Children aren't sleepy, Mugs of Cocoa they carry
They're waiting for Christmas, the Young and the Old
But do they remember the story that was told?

It's not about boxes, ribbons and such
But about a Savior who loved us so much
He left His glory far away, up on high
And came down to earth to save men, by and by

But today we celebrate the birth of this King
Whom the Shepherds did visit and the angels did sing
The Wise Men did travel following His Star
Brought gifts of gold and myrrh and frankincense in a jar

They had learned from the scrolls written long ago
That Jesus would come dwell on earth here below
He was born in a stable and laid on fresh hay
And this was the very first Christmas day

The Angel told Joseph and Mary, you see
Of the child she would carry and how special He would be
That they should love and care for Him as their own
Though He would one day as the Son of God be known

All of these secrets Mary held deep in her heart
And pondered them often from the very start
Together they raised God come to earth
And Wise Men and Women still honor His birth

~*~

"So they hurried off and found Mary and Joseph, and the baby, who
was lying in the manger. When they had seen him, they spread the
word concerning what had been told them about this child, and all
who heard it were amazed at what the shepherds said to them. But
Mary treasured up all these things and pondered them in her heart.
The shepherds returned, glorifying and praising God for all the things
they had heard and seen, which were just as they had been told."-
Luke 2:16-20 NIV

Wise Men STILL Seek Him!

The Road To Bethlehem

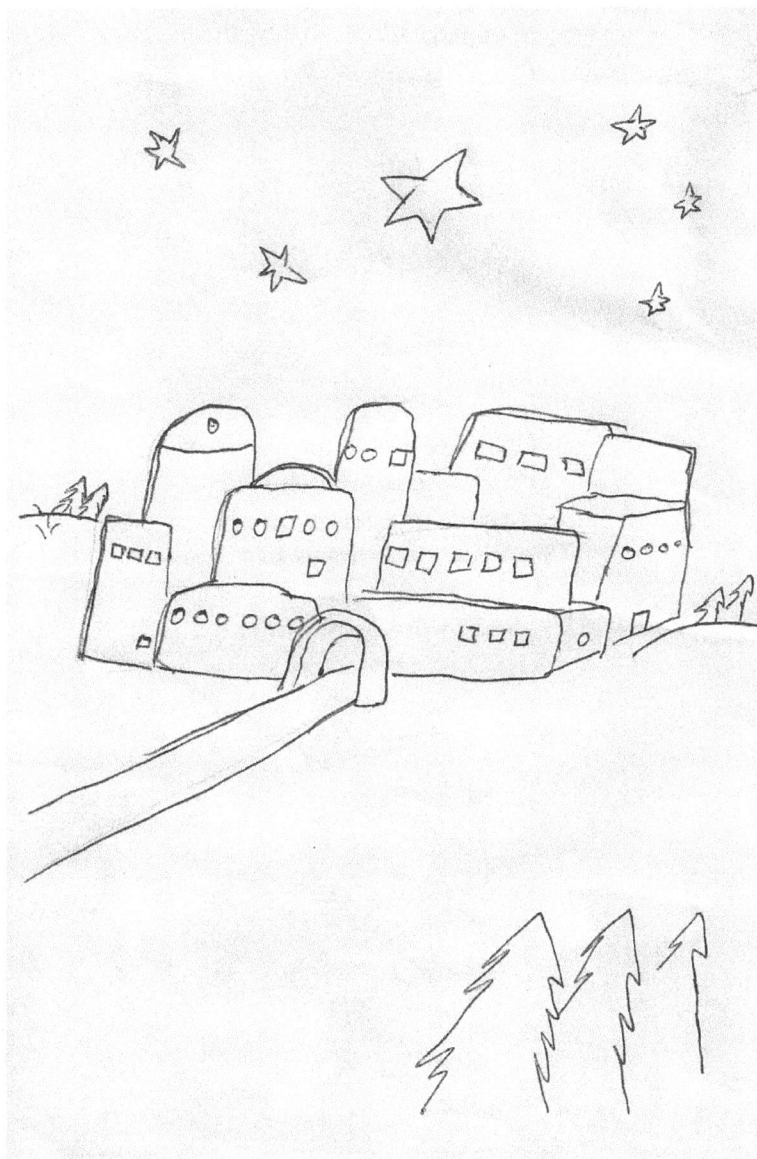

The Road to Bethlehem

We took the road to Bethlehem
My beloved and me
For Cesar had a census called
A new tax had decreed

From Galilee the road was harsh
We walked along the way
Traveling in a caravan
To keep the thieves at bay

In Bethlehem the crowds grew thick
The inns turned us away
There was no place to make a bed
Save a manger in the hay

My love was soon to bear a Son
A Child of Holy birth
The One of whom Isaiah told
Would one day come to earth

We made a bed within a barn
The animals' gave us room
A bed of hay, sweet and clean
A bright starry sky drive away the gloom

The road to Bethlehem we took
Late one starry night
The angels came and sang a song
God's glory gave them Light

The song they sang told a tale
Of a New King come to earth
A baby born in Bethlehem
And of His lowly birth

They sent us down to tell the crowds
Of the Savior God did send
We left the sheep there on the hill
To take the road to Bethlehem

The angels' song led to a cave
Where ox and donkey lay
The manger were they ate their feed
Was where our New King played

When we found the resting place
Of the Savior come to earth
Our hearts were filled with peace and love
Our souls were filled with mirth

We shared the news of Jesus birth
With those who filled the street
We told them all of the King of Kings
Who slept among the sheep

We took the road from Bethlehem
Back up the darkened hills
To join the sheep and get some sleep
Our hearts with joy he fills

~*~

We took the road to Bethlehem
To follow a shining star
The prophets told in stories old
Of a King to be born a far

The journey on the road to Bethlehem
Was fraught with toilsome days
We traveled by night to see the star's light
'Twas our guide all along the way

A caravan of traveling kings
From the east we came
To greet the King whose star we'd seen
And we shed abroad His fame

To the holy city of peace we came
Of the new King to inquire
But the magistrate became irate
When we told of this new Sire

The court astrologers came to tell
Of the Messiah long foretold
And of the star that would guide the way
With a light for all to behold

They told the king that Bethlehem
Was the place where the child lay
The king relayed this news to us
And sent us on our way

But in the night while following the light
The Lord did warn our hearts
And told us to go and visit the child
But in another direction to depart

The star did stop above a home
Upon a Bethlehem street
We followed it right up to the door
The new King we came to greet

The mother did invite us in
The father standing guard
We took our gifts inside the house
While our camels filled their yard

Within the home we open our chests
Our presents to present
Bags of gold and jars of myrrh
And vials of frankincense

Precious gifts of greatest worth
To honor the King of Kings
God's only Son has come to earth
Salvation to us He brings

We took the road from Bethlehem
Across the continent
The angel's warning we did heed
And another direction we went

~*~

We took the road from Bethlehem
To Egypt we did flee
My beautiful bride, the baby fair
The king's gifts, and me

We lived among strangers there
The child's life to save
When God sent His angel to bring us home
I fear I was not brave

The king who sought to kill the child
Had passed away and yet
His family was still upon the throne
Which caused my heart to fret

We turned aside to Galilee
To Nazareth town we moved
Back to the place were we began
The home that we had loved

~*~

The Roman world does believe
That all roads lead to Rome
And yet we find through these tails here
This is not true for some

These travelers to Bethlehem
Forever changed the earth
For they all have played an important part
In the story of Salvations' birth.

~*~

Happy Birthday Jesus
And
Merry Christmas!

The Christian Walk

J O Y

Jesus is the source of true joy.
Putting Him first in your life
Is the way to start having His joy.

Others also need joy.
Teaching them of Jesus and how to
Follow Him is the next step on the path to
true joy.

You are the next link in this chain of joy.
You must take time out of your busy
schedule for yourself. Pamper yourself
with time well spent in His Word and
prayer to be fully grounded in His JOY!

~*~

Yet I will rejoice in the Lord, I will joy in
The God of my salvation. Habakkuk 3:18

Never Alone!

From the day I came
With You to abide
You have always been there
Close by my side

When I stumble and fall,
Or skin up my knee
You are always there
Ready to comfort me

If I choose a path
That leads me astray
Your Light in my darkness
Shows me the way

Or, when I'm afraid
And crying in the dark
You're right there beside me,
Your Love to impart

Never alone,
With You I will be
You are closer than
My very breath is to me

~*~

Then shalt thou call, and the Lord shall
Answer; Thou shalt cry, and He shall say,
Here am I. Isaiah 58:9

Let your conversation be without covetousness;
And be content with such things as ye have:
For he hath said, I will never leave thee,
Nor forsake thee. So that we may boldly say,
The Lord is my helper, and I will not fear what
Man shall do unto me. Hebrews 13:5-6

Only You

Only You hear the cry of my heart.
Only You heal my soul,
Take my fear and pain away.

Only You can fill me with joy.
Only with You is where I always want to stay.

Only You hear the cry of my heart.
Only You leave Your comfort
With Your Holy Spirit, who stays.

Only You can make me complete.
Only with You is where I always want to
stay.

It's only with You.
It's only with You.
It's only with You!

~*~

Wherefore seeing we also are compassed about
With so great a cloud of witnesses, let us lay
Aside every weight, and the sin which doth so
Easily beset us, and let us run with patience the
Race that is set before us, Looking unto Jesus
The author and finisher of our faith; who for the
Joy that was set before him endured the cross,
Despising the shame, and is set down at the right
Hand of the throne of God. Hebrews 13:1, 2

Jesus' Prayer

Before He died on Calvary
Jesus prayed for you and me
That to this world we would not hold
But long to walk on streets of gold

To value His purity within
And ever seek to be free from sin
To share His love along the way
And sing His praises every day

Lord, may we be like the prayer You prayed
That we may ever like You be arrayed
In garments pure and white as snow
That others may Your reflection know
And seek to find what we have found
A life where Your peace and grace do abound

~*~

And now I am no more in the world, but these are in the
world, and I come to thee, Holy Father, keep through Thine
own Name those whom Thou hast given Me, that they may be
one, as We are. John 17:11

Rejoice

Rejoice, for I am with you
Rejoice, and walk in Peace
Reach out your hands
And grasp onto Me

Rejoice, for I am with you
Rejoice. Step out in Love
Rejoice, there's freedom waiting
When your hope is above

Rejoice, for I am with you
Rejoice, the healing's near
Rejoice, deliverance happens
Bondage disappears

Rejoice, for I am with you
Rejoice. Be not over come
Rejoice, the darkness leaves you
When you shine with the Son

Rejoice, for I am with you
Rejoice. Be free today
Rejoice, the new is come
The old is passed away

Rejoice, for I am with you
Rejoice, and fear no more
Rejoice. Walk on in me
Through each new door

REJOICE!

~*~

Rejoice in the Lord always:
And again I say, Rejoice.
Philippians 4:4

True Joy

But let those that put their trust in thee
rejoice: let them ever shout for joy,
because thou defendest them: let them
also that love thy name be joyful in thee.
For thou, Lord, wilt bless the righteous;
with favor wilt thou compass him as with
a shield. Psalm 5:11-12

Yes, Lord in You is true joy. And as I sit
reading this verse I am reminded of a
plaque on the wall of a long ago attended
Sunday school room. It simply said:

Jesus

Others

You

So profound in all of it's simplicity, Lord;
but I have found this is quite true in my
own life. As I put Jesus first in my life and
others ahead of myself I am filled with joy.
True JOY, that only You can give!

~*~

If ye keep my commandments, ye shall abide in my love; Even as I
have kept my Father's commandments, and abide in His love. These
things have I spoken unto you, that My joy might remain in you, and
that your joy might be full. This is My commandment, that ye love
one another, as I have loved you. John 15:10-12

J O Y

Jesus is the source of true joy.
Putting Him first in your life
Is the way to start having His joy.

Others also need joy.
Teaching them of Jesus and how to
Follow Him is the next step on the path to
true joy.

You are the next link in this chain of joy.
You must take time out of your busy
schedule for yourself. Pamper yourself
with time well spent in His Word and
prayer to be fully grounded in His JOY!

~*~

Yet I will rejoice in the Lord,
I will joy in The God of my salvation.
Habakkuk 3:18

What a Love

As I look across the deep, blue sky
I begin to wonder why
That God gave His Son to die
Oh what a Love for you and I

And as I see the flowers bloom
I know that God alone must groom
This beauty seen by passersby
Oh what a Love for you and I

All this I see and often sigh
That others have not questioned why
An innocent Man bled and died
To save such a one as you or I

Do they not see the deep, blue sky
Or the flowers that bloom nearby?
Are we keeping this Love hidden inside
This Love He shared with you and I?

Such a Love we'll never quite know
That to the cross He'd gladly go
Wounded and bleeding there to die
This wonderful Love for You and I

~*~

For God so loved the world, that he gave His only begotten Son, that whosoever believeth in him should not perish, but have everlasting life. John 3:16

For he whom God hath sent speaketh the words of God: for God giveth not the Spirit by measure unto him. The Father loveth The Son, and hath given all things into his hand. He that believeth on the Son hath everlasting life: and he that believeth not The Son shall not see life; but the wrath of God abideth on him. John 3:34-36

God's Gifts

Forgiveness
is His gift of Love
He gave upon the tree

Salvation
He brought without a doubt,
By the blood He shed for we

Grace
His unearned favor He pours out
on you and me

Mercy
is the gift He gave
as from our sins He set us free

May all of these abound in us,
as we wander through each day
Sharing with others the gifts of Jesus
And growing in our faith

~*~

If ye then, being evil, know how to give
Good gifts unto your children, how much
More shall your Father which is in heaven
Give good gifts unto them that ask Him?
                        Matthew 7:11

G R A C E

<u>G</u>od
<u>R</u>ighteously
<u>A</u>bsolving the
<u>C</u>onsequences of sin for
<u>E</u>very true believer in Christ!

~*~

" . . .This is the true grace of God,
Stand fast in it."
I Peter 5:12 NIV

Grace

Grace, Grace
Abundant and free
Grace, Grace
Poured out on me

You gave up Your life
To ransom my soul
To pardon completely
And make me whole

Your Grace I've accepted
Your Mercy, let in
Thanks to You my heart
Is now free from sin

Unmerited favor
Sent from above
Flows unto me
From Your heart of Love

May I with others
Share this great Grace
And prepare them for glory
And the smile on Your face!

~*~

For by grace are ye saved through faith;
and that not of yourselves; it is the gift of
God: not of works, lest any man should
boast. Eph 2:8-9

Thank You, Lord

Lord, thank You
For Your quiet touch
To me it means so very much

A gentle prodding of the heart
Guiding me,
While Your grace You impart

A quiet prayer, a gentle touch
A soft word spoken
All mean so much

When offered with Your precious Love
And following Your guidance
Sent from above

May I ever be open to hear Your voice
That I may touch others
And You may rejoice

~*~

"In everything give thanks, for this is the
Will of God in Christ Jesus concerning you."
I Thessalonians 5:18

Look For The Light

Look for the Light
It's brighter than the sun
'Tis our blessed Jesus
God's Only Begotten One

He made a way in darkness
To take away all sin
Just open up your heart
And truly let Him in

He Lights the path before us
And leads us all the way
And He will reign victorious
On that Blessed Day

Let Jesus Light-up your darkness
And walk into that land
Where men will live in harmony
And Lion will lay with Lamb

~*~

"In HIM was life and the life was
the LIGHT of men." John 1:9

Peace With Jesus

Jesus said He was leaving His peace with
us. And He did just that. For Jesus is the
Prince of Peace. His very essence is the
peace we feel when we are in right
relationship with Him. He fills us with
this peace when we become His children.

He promised to leave us a comforter,
which He fulfilled when he gave us the
gift of his Holy Spirit. HIS spirit indwells
each of us at the moment of our conversion.

In Isaiah 9:6 and Eph 2:14 it
says He is our peace. And this He will
Always Be, as long as we follow the path
He has chosen for us to follow throughout
our lives. Lets be at Peace, with Jesus.

Peace I leave with you, my peace I give
unto you: not as the world giveth, give I
unto you. Let not your heart be troubled,
neither let it be afraid. John 14:27

Yes, Lord, Your peace is beyond
Understanding. You fill me with calm in
The midst of my struggles and show me
The path through them. I may never be
Without problems in this world. But, You
Have promised to direct my ways and give
Me Your peace. Thank you, precious
Lord!

~*~

And the peace of God, which passeth all
Understanding, shall keep your hearts
And minds through Christ Jesus.
Philippians 4:7

Peace

Peace
Precious peace
That comforts the soul

Enduring
Forever
and making me whole

Abiding
Within me
Faithful and true

Christ
My Savior,
It is only YOU

Echoing
From within me
Whenever I speak

Sharing with others
This Peace that they seek

~*~

Peace I leave with you, My peace I give
Unto you: not as the world giveth, give I
Unto you. Let not your heart be troubled,
Neither let it be afraid. Psalms 14:27

Holy

Lord, let me ever holy be
Becoming more and more like Thee

Daily walking by Your side
And happy with You to abide

Following each of Your commands
Never to be plucked from Your mighty hand

Becoming ever more like thee
Lord let me ever holy be!

~*~

Because it is written, be ye holy; for I am holy.
1Peter 1:16

~*~

I beseech you therefore, brethren,
By the mercies of God, that ye present
Your bodies a living sacrifice, holy, acceptable
Unto God, which is your reasonable service.
Romans 12:1

The Glory Of The Lord

Oh the glory of the Lord that shines
When the tongues of men spit upon him
Oh the blessings He affords
The servants bearing this within

They stand beneath its heavy weight
But, Jesus will lift it at heaven's gate
This burden lasts but a short while
When compared to the length
of His loving smile

May His smile NEVER quit,
No matter how much men may spit!

~*~

If ye be reproached for the name of
Christ, happy are ye; for the Spirit of
Glory and of God resteth upon you: or
Their part He is evil spoken of, but on
Your part He is glorified.
I Peter 4:14

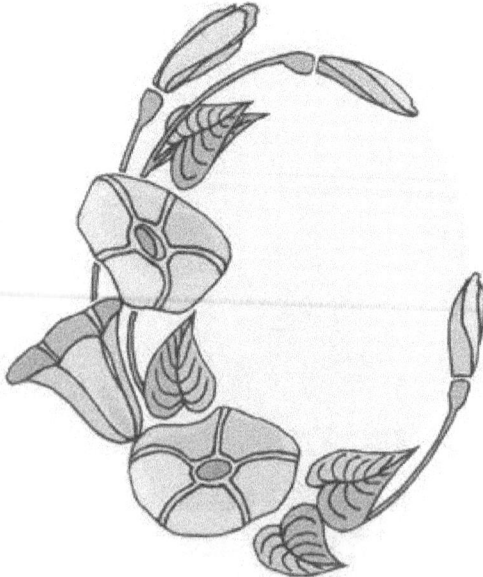

Holiness

Holiness is what You require
And to Your holiness, I dare to aspire
Set apart for service to You
Ready to do all You desire

Prepare me, Oh Lord
For what lies ahead
And teach me to trod
Only where You tread

I am Your servant
I'll follow Your way
When I open my mouth
I will say what You say

For holiness is what You require
And Your holiness is my only desire

~*~

Wherefore come out from among them, and be ye separate, saith the Lord, and touch not the unclean thing; and I will receive you. And will be a Father unto you, and ye shall be My sons and daughters, saith the Lord Almighty. Having therefore these promises, dearly beloved, let us cleanse ourselves from all filthiness of the flesh and spirit, perfecting holiness in the fear of God. 2 Corinthians 6:17-7:1

Thank You For Being My Friend

Thank you, Lord
For being my friend
For traveling with me
'til the journey's end

For walking beside me
Your hand in mine
Showing me where to go
And that at its proper time

You're the Great Leader
And You comfort my soul
Ever beside me
All the way to our goal

Thank you, Lord Jesus
For being my friend
And traveling with me
'Til the journey's end

~*~

Greater love hath no man than this, that a man lay down his life for his friends. Ye are my friends, if ye do whatsoever I command you. Henceforth I call you not servants; for the servant knoweth not what His lord doeth: but I have called you friends; for all things that I have heard of my Father I have made known unto you.
John 15:13-15

Love's Healing

Life brings broken heartedness
LOVE brings healing in your breast

The power of the cross
Defeats all your loss

And brings about a brilliant gloss . . .
. . . On the gemstone that is you

Broken heartedness heals
And True Love reveals

Christ's presence and power
Within you IS Real!

~*~

And the apostles, when they were returned, told him all that they had done. And he took them, and went aside privately into a desert Place belonging to the city called Bethsaida. And the people, when they knew it, followed Him: and he received them, and spake unto Them of the kingdom of God, and healed them that had need of healing. Luke 9:10-11

Balm of Gilead

There is a healing for the soul
It is the balm of Gilead
A quietness and peace below
Like none I ever had
Come give peace unto my heart
And from Your rest I'll ne're depart
I'll carry it with me
Where e're I go
And others lead to its peaceful flow
Balm of Gilead so sweet
Heal me as I sit at Jesus' feet

~*~

Babylon is suddenly fallen and destroyed:
Howl for her; take balm for her pain,
If so be she may be healed. Jeremiah 51:8

Surely he hath borne our griefs, and carried our sorrows: yet we did
esteem him stricken, smitten of God, and afflicted. But he was
wounded for our transgressions, he was bruised for our iniquities: the
chastisement of our peace was upon him; and with his stripes we are
healed. Isaiah 53:4, 5

Purity

Lord I long with You to dwell
And face to face to see
The wonders of Your matchless grace
And all Your love for me

And yet I know 'tis only
With a heart of purity
That anyone may look upon
Your wondrous fair beauty

And so I seek to be made pure
Of heart and mind and soul
That when I get to heaven fair
Your face in beauty I'll behold

~*~

"Blessed are the pure in heart; for they
Shall see God." Matthew 5:8

Rebuke not an elder, but intreat him as a father; and the younger men as brethren; the elder women as mothers; the younger as sisters, with all purity.

1Timothy 5:1, 2

These things command and teach. Let no man despise thy youth; but be thou an example of the believers, in word, in conversation, in charity, in spirit, in Faith, in purity. Till I come, give attendance to reading, to Exhortation, to doctrine. 1 Timothy 4:11-13

God's Generosity

You are constantly giving more
Than I could ever know

Pouring out Your gifts
For me on others to bestow

No matter how much I give out
Never shall I lack

For as I spoon them out the front door
You shovel more in the back!

~*~

Now he who supplies seed to the sower and bread for food will also supply and increase your store of seed and will enlarge the harvest of your righteousness. You will be made rich in every way so that you can be generous on every occasion, and through us your generosity will result in thanksgiving to God. This service that you perform is not only supplying the needs of God's people but is also overflowing in many expressions of thanks to God. 2 Corinthians 9:10-12 NIV

G E N E R O U S

Giving freely

Enjoying the feeling

Never without our needs met

Ever seeking where to bless

Receiver of His very best

Overflowing with peace and love

United with our Lord above

Serving Him where ever we go

For He is more generous than we know!

~*~

Remember this: whoever sows sparingly
Will also reap sparingly, and whoever
Sows generously will also reap generously.
II Corinthians 9:6 NIV

Forgiveness

Forgiveness is a gift,
We to ourselves must give
When others against us have transgressed
With heaviness we get depressed
And loose Christ's freedom from our breast
Which makes it hard with Him to live

But when we allow forgiveness in
This frees us from our path of sin
Again become we whole and clean
Lord may our hearts forever be
To lead transgressors back to Thee
That we may in harmony live
Our praises unto Thee to give

Forgiveness is not just for the sake of the person who has transgressed against you. It is also to free your spirit and to put you into right relationship with the true Forgiver, Jesus.

~*~

Forgive us our debts, as we also have forgiven our debtors. And lead us not into temptation, but deliver us from the evil one. For if you forgive men when they sin against you, your heavenly Father will also forgive you. But if you do not forgive men their Sins, your Father will not forgive your sins. Luke 6:12-15 NIV

The Lord is slow to anger, abounding in
love and forgiving sin and rebellion.
Numbers 14:18 NIV

Seeking God's Guidance

While waiting in your "upper room"
For guidance from above
Remember, we're all there with you
In Spirit and in Love

The Spirit of God abides in us
And we're in one accord
When we meet with Him in worship
That sweet communion with our Lord

~*~

And hope maketh not ashamed, because
The love of God is shed abroad in our
Hearts by the Holy Ghost which is given
Unto us. Romans 5:5

But this is that which is spoken
Of by the prophet Joel. Acts 2:16

Guidance

<u>G</u>OD YO<u>U</u> AND <u>I</u> <u>DANCE</u>

I promise I'll let You lead!

~*~

The proverbs of Solomon son of David,
King of Israel: for attaining wisdom and discipline;
For understanding words of insight;
For acquiring a disciplined and prudent life,
Doing what is right and just and fair;
For giving prudence to the simple,
Knowledge and discretion to the young
Let the wise listen and add to their learning,
And let the discerning get guidance
For understanding proverbs and parables,
The sayings and riddles of the wise
The fear of the LORD is the beginning of knowledge,
But fools despise wisdom and discipline.
Proverbs 1:1-7

Self-control
(Temperance)

Self-control is a gift God
Grants us from above
We cannot do it on our own,
He sends it wrapped up in His love

As we unwrap His gift of Love
And hold it close within
This gift of God blooms in our heart
And stays our soul from sin

For gluttony is a sin
Which comes forth in many ways
But walking in His gift of love doth keep
This sin at bay

For self-control is a gift
God plants within our heart
The more we walk forth in His love
The bigger grows it's part

By practicing the gifts God gives
Surely you must see
When we arrive at home on high
Abundant they shall be!

~*~

But the fruit of the Spirit is love, joy,
Peace, longsuffering, gentleness, goodness,
Faith, meekness, temperance: against such
There is no law. Galatians 5:22-23

Servant

A servant He was
So a servant I shall be
That in Him I may dwell
Throughout eternity
He is my perfect example
Of how a man should live
Washing the feet of others
And never afraid to give
Thank You, precious Savior
For showing me the way
To have my sins forgiven
And live with You every day

~*~

"Who being in the form of God, thought
it not robbery to be equal with God: But
made Himself of no reputation, and took
upon Him the form of a servant, and was
made in the likeness of men."
Philippians 2:6,7

GREATNESS

Many find greatness in those who have made a name for themselves in some way; be it sports, politics, the arts or the multi-faceted media industry. Jesus' disciples were arguing among themselves as to which of them was the greatest. His answer to them is His reply to us, as well: *At that time the disciples came to Jesus and asked, "Who is the greatest in the kingdom of heaven?" He called a little child and had him stand among them. And he said: "I tell you the truth, unless you change and become like little children, you will never enter the kingdom of heaven. Therefore, whoever humbles himself like this child is the greatest in the kingdom of heaven. And whoever welcomes a little child like this in my name welcomes me." Matthew 18:1-5 NIV*

~*~

Godly

Reverent and Respectful

Edifying others

Attuned to the Holy Spirit

Trusting and Trustworthy

New birth in Jesus

Everlasting life

Satisfied with such as he has

Servant of ALL!

~*~

The greatest among you will be your servant.
For whoever exalts himself will be humbled,
and whoever humbles himself will be exalted.
Matthew 23:11-12

S E R V A N T

Silent life of Sacrifice
Every thought for those around you
Rightly dividing His words of truth
Victorious in battles with sin and self
Abundant life of joy and peace through trials
Never seeking glory or honor of men
Totally surrendered to Jesus and a life of
   Giving to others for Him and His Glory

Servanthood is NOT slavery. It is merely placing the needs of others before your own. Jesus thought that the place of a servant was the greatest position in His whole kingdom.

~*~

But ye shall not be so: But he that is greatest among you, let him Be as the younger; and he that is chief, as He that doth serve. For whether is greater, He that sitteth at meat, or he that serveth? Is not he that sitteth at meat? But I am among you as he that serveth.
Luke 22:26-27

He riseth from supper, and laid aside his garments; and took a towel, and girded himself. After that he Poureth water into a basin, and began to wash the disciples' feet, and to wipe them with the towel wherewith he was girded. ... So after he had washed their feet, and had taken his garments, and was set down again, he said unto them, Know ye what I have done to you? Ye call me Master and Lord: and ye say well; for so I am. If I then, your Lord and Master, have washed your feet; ye also ought to wash one another's feet. For I have given you an example, that ye should do as I have done to you. Verily, verily, I say unto you, The servant is not greater than his lord; neither he that is sent greater than he that sent him. If ye know these things, happy are ye if ye do them. John 13:4, 5

A Missionary's Heart

Wherever I go whatever I may say
May my words touch a heart unsaved each day
May a drop of truth open their hearts and minds
May they all repent and true Salvation find
Oh that hell were an empty place
Where no man would ever go
And that un-repentance would never be
The condition of even one soul
May Christ's forgiveness ever be
My message through the years
And many lead to Jesus' side
Through laughter, joy and tears
That I may see all those I meet
The path to heaven trod
That we may all sit at Jesus' feet
And forever live with God

As young high school student I attended my first Missionary conference; the David Lyon Family had returned from Senegal, Africa. They told stories of the lives they had touched with the Gospel and of those lives that had changed them, too. I was hooked; someday I was going to some far place and reach lost souls for Jesus. Many years have passed since that long ago day but I have never left my home country for any reason. Yet I still long to teach others of our Lord and Savior. God has seen fit to send the words He's given and the lessons I've learned to those far away fields to reach hurting souls and lead them to the Healer of hearts and lives, King Jesus! I still have the heart of a missionary, but my field is reached by printed pages and Internet sites. Praise God for His diversity of methods. The message will always be the same, Jesus Christ and Him crucified.

A Patient Spirit

Proud we are when we come to Jesus
We think, "We can do it all."
Then He beckons us on higher
With His gentle call.

Higher, higher He does lead us,
Closer to His side
Teaching us faith, hope and joy.
Breaking down our walls of pride.

Patience is a blessed virtue,
Conquering all of our sin
Till it has its 'perfect work'
Dwelling with us deep within

Once our voice did bellow out,
'Hey come and look at me!'
But as we draw closer to Jesus,
We hope they see 'none but Thee.'

Once a proud and boastful lot
We began this road to trod
Now we humbly seek to be
More and more like God

'Patience is her own reward,'
These words are ever true
For Your patience, Thank You, Lord
May we ever be like You!

~*~

The end of a thing is better than its
Beginning; the patient in spirit is better than
The proud in spirit. Ecclesiastes 7:8

Winter of the Heart

Winter of the Heart

Winter is not just a season;
It can be a season of the heart
When the cold shoulder rolls,
And all friendliness departs

Children of the Lord
Should ne're permit it in
For coldness to another
From His chosen ones is sin

We are to be welcoming
To others, in His name
Bidding them to enter in
And His Salvation claim

If attitude of the heart
Should to a season be compared
The 'new life' of springtime
Should be its weather fair

For this should be our goal in life,
When bringing others to the Lord
That all may share eternity
With Him, forever more

~*~

Cold and winter of our hearts can spring from many things; death of
a loved one or a marriage and even prolonged illness. It is
understandable and even permissible – for a time. But when grieving
is ended and self-pity has run its course, we need to again seek our joy
in Jesus our Lord.

~*~

For his anger endureth but a moment; in his favor is life: weeping
may endure for a night, but joy cometh in the morning. Psalm 30:5

Wisdom

Wisdom of the Lord is sweet
May we gain more every day
And never from it's way retreat
But strengthen our hold come what may
To be more like You would be so sweet
Let us not from Your wisdom e're retreat

~*~

Thank You, Lord for imparting
Your wisdom when ours is so vain
May we ever seek after her
And make true wisdom our friend.

~*~

God has always encouraged His people to seek wisdom; both Old and
New Testament passages bear this out. Our Lord doesn't want
anyone to lack any good thing, and wisdom is a very good thing. He is
a giver of good gifts, all we have to do is ask – seek – these gifts from
His hand open them and put them to use in our lives.

~*~

Get wisdom, get understanding: forget it Not; neither decline from the
words of my mouth. Forsake her not, and she shall preserve thee: love
her, and she shall keep thee. Wisdom is the principle thing; therefore
get wisdom: and with all thy getting get understanding.
Proverbs 4:5-7

If any of you lack wisdom, let him ask of God, that giveth to all men
liberally, and upbraideth not; and it shall be given him. But let him
ask in faith, nothing wavering. For he that wavereth is like a wave of
the sea driven with the wind and tossed. James 1:5-6

H O P E

Holding on when others have already let go.

Obediently believing the words of Jesus;
   "I will never leave you nor forsake you."

Perfect Peace; especially in the darkest
   nights or roughest storms.

Expecting an answer, even if I must wait
   till I see Him face to face.

~*~

Hope is much more than a weak word that maybe something good
and right will happen to us. It is a reality that we can <u>know </u>our
expectations <u>in Jesus</u> will truly be fulfilled. He will bring about
everything He has promised – for it is already set into motion, and no
one can stop it!

~*~

I have set the LORD always before me: because he is at my right
hand, I shall not be moved. Therefore my heart is glad, and my glory
rejoiceth: my flesh also shall rest in hope. Psalm 16:8-9 KJV

"Wherefore gird up the loins of your
mind, be sober, and HOPE to the end for
the grace that is to be brought unto you at
the revelation of Jesus" 1 Peter 1:13 KJV

Two Paths

Before me lay two paths and chose I must
How will I know which way to trust?
To the left lay heartache, struggle and pain.
To the right lay joy in a life "born again"
Show me Your path, Lord. Teach me Your ways.
And I shall follow You all of my days!

~*~

Every person, young and old must choose
The life they will live; will it be a holy life
As desired by God our Lord and Savior?
Or will it be a life of selfishness, living
Only to seek life's pleasures? Jesus desires
Us all, but he didn't create a set of mindless
Robots, He gave us hearts and minds and
The freedom of choice. And God is a gentleman.
He will never force anyone to choose the path
of Grace. He calls to us and waits patiently for
us to answer. Then He shows us the way home.

~*~

Thou wilt shew me the path of Life: in
Thy presence is fullness of joy; at Thy
Right hand there are pleasures for
Evermore. Psalm 16:11

~*~

"Don't look for shortcuts to God. The market is flooded with surefire,
easygoing formulas for a successful life that can be practiced in your
spare time. Don't fall for that stuff, even though crowds of people do.
The way to life - to God! - is vigorous and requires total attention.
Matthew 7:13-14 The Message Bible.

To Be Like Jesus

Oh to be like You,
Lord, in every way
To know exactly what to do,
The perfect words to say

If we are ever seeking
To see the face of God
Then as we closer draw to Him,
His pathway we will trod

As we walk like Jesus
In this world below
The lives we have touched will feel
The Holy Spirit's glow

His presence is within us,
Perfecting us inside
So when life's trials rage without,
In Jesus we can hide

Constantly abiding,
'Tis all I want to be
Closer still to Jesus
For all eternity

May I dwell beside You
Today and evermore
And be with You forever,
On that Happy Golden Shore!

~*~

Abide in me, and I in you. As the branch cannot bear fruit of itself, except it abide in the vine; no more can ye, except ye abide in me. I am the vine, ye are the branches: He that abideth in me, and I in him, the same bringeth forth much fruit: for without me ye can do nothing. If a man abide not in me, he is cast forth as a branch, and is withered; and men gather them, and cast them into the fire, And they are burned. If ye abide in me, and my Words abide in you, ye shall ask what ye will, and it shall be done unto you. John 15:4-8

I Have Come – Help Me Learn

I have come to love You,
I have come to love You,
I have come to love You,
Help me learn to love You.

I have come to serve You,
I have come to serve You,
I have come to serve You,
Help me learn to serve You.

I have come to worship You,
I have come to worship You,
I have come to worship You,
Help me learn to worship You.

I have come to follow You,
I have come to follow You,
I have come to follow You,
Help me learn to follow You.

I have come to praise You,
I have come to praise You,
I have come to praise You,
Help me learn to praise You.

I have come to love You,
I have come to love You,
I have come to love You,
Help me learn to love You

~*~

God's Spirit draws us to Jesus, but our reformation and regeneration is not instantaneous. It takes time to learn just what is required in our new life with Jesus. We need to knock and keep knocking, seek and keep seeking and to ask and keep right on asking what Jesus Wants from and for each of us!

~*~

Ask, and it shall be given you; seek, and ye shall find; knock, and it shall be opened unto you: For every one that asketh receiveth; and he that seeketh findeth; and to him that knocketh it shall be opened.
Matthew 7:7-8

Following Jesus

"Be ye perfect as I am perfect." This is
One of Jesus' commands to us. And as we
Follow closely to Jesus we learn what this
"Perfection" is all about. It is a maturity
And completeness that we cannot gain in
A lifestyle that doesn't include the Master.
But one in which we each follow our own
Path, the path He has chosen for us.

The Bible says, "there is a way that
Seemeth right unto a man, but the ends
Thereof are the ways of destruction." So if
We choose to follow our own way it will
Lead us to death, which is complete and
Total separation from Jesus. Today, and
Everyday, you have the choice to follow
Jesus . . . or yourself. Choose Wisely!

I will follow Jesus!

~*~

Whoever serves Me must follow Me; and
Where I am, My servant also will be. My
Father will honor the one who serves Me.
John 12:26

The Waters of Life

A quiet stream where I sit
And ponder life,
The meaning of it
Deep it flows and shallow too,
Reflecting His Light
And His life
Richness dwells in waters deep
While rippling shallows
Wash away strife
Its quiet voice calms the mind
Leading me to wander
Where the ripples roll
Nourishing pools add to the growth
Which gives shade to the body
And rest to the soul

~*~

I really draw strength from Psalms 23, for when I am having a difficult struggle I find a quiet place in God's outdoors by a lake or stream where I can sit and contemplate things. Often I give a private concert to Him while sitting amongst all His wonderful beauty and wilderness.

~*~

He maketh me to lie down in green pastures: he leadeth me beside the still waters. He restoreth my soul: he leadeth me in the paths of righteousness for his name's sake. Psalms 23:2, 3.

Waters of Life

Baptism

This is a public declaration of what You
have done in my life and the lives of all
believers. It is a statement of faith; our faith
in You, Lord. Leaving the Old ways of life
behind and following You in newness of
life. A life of freedom from the past, from
besetting sins, from darkness and dismay.
A life full of Your Light that shines into
the deepest recesses of my mind, heart,
and my very soul.

Baptism is a way to tell the world I belong
to You. It is also a marker; a milestone
with a date attached that I can look back
on when doubt begins to creep in. And a
beacon of all that is to come that I can
look forward to with anticipation. Mine
was July 4, 2004. Thank You, Lord for this
Burial marker with its date – this spiritual
Headstone that I can revisit whenever I need to!

~*~

We are therefore buried with Him through baptism into death in
order that, just as Christ was raised from the dead through the glory
of the Father, we too may live a new life. Romans 6:4 NIV

The Heart of a Child

In the heart of a child lie qualities rare
An eagerness to learn yet without despair
Wonderment at the ways of life quite unique
And a willingness to explore all the ground 'neath their feet
A trusting heart and a ready smile
These too lay within the heart of a child

But once in a while a child's heart is torn
He is hurt in his soul and his spirit is forlorn
He turns into a skeptic, his heart in pieces, broken
All this is because of the lies Satan has spoken
"God is dead," he's been told, "he doesn't exist
"You're all alone now," and there goes his bliss

This in very tale I speak of a child, 'tis true
But this could very easily be me or you
For each of us is the child of the King
He made us and bought us His praises to sing
But our enemy lies and brings us such doubt
He puts cracks in our armor and drains our faith out

We've neglected the upkeep our spirit deserves
Forgotten our prayer time and shelved God's word
When we came to Jesus, we trusted with such joy
But along the way our 'childlikeness' became void
We hastened to 'grow-up' and be more mature
But, we did it 'our way' not His, that's for sure

When we act 'all grown up' we forget who's the Boss
We allow Satan to run rampant within all our thoughts
He whispers such innocent sounding things in our ears
But that we actually believe him is the thing that I fear
For Satan is a liar and the father of all lies
By listening to him he steals all of our joy by and by.

But Jesus will forgive our mistakes and our sins
We have to repent and allow His presence back in
He will clean up our heart and restore all our faith
When we've repented He floods us again with His grace

He restores our childlike nature and all those qualities rare
He renews our wonderment and removes all despair

Again we come unto Him again with the heart of a child
Our spirits will be trusting and our face filled with smiles
He will open our eyes if we ask Him to see
All the disguises of Satan and the attacks that may be
Jesus will also teach us to stand firm and strong
So that when time is over we'll be a part of His throng

So hold your childlike nature deep within your heart
And stay close to Jesus, let Him never depart
Let Him sing the songs of Heaven by a whisper in your ear
So the attacks of Satan you won't so easily hear
And when you see others of Jesus drowning in despair
Direct them into His outstretched arms for a dose of His loving care

Like a Child

Simple in faith and expectant of heart
This is the place where true life does start

Growing in stature and also in grace
With the Light of Your love upon his face

A child of God, this new babe in Christ
Walking Your pathway, ever so bright

Full of wonder at all that he sees
Yet longing to dwell ever closer to thee

Reading, believing, accepting Your word
Soaking up like a sponge all that he's heard

Unafraid and filled with such awe
Truly excited about his new life in God

We veterans of faith, ever should seek
To be more like this child as we used to be

Full of Your wonder and clothed in Your grace
Eagerly, expectantly seeking Your face!

~*~

But Jesus called them unto him, and said, suffer little children to come unto me, and forbid them not: for of such is the kingdom of God. Verily I say unto you, whosoever shall not receive the kingdom of God as a little child shall in no wise enter therein. Luke 18-16, 17.

Mariposas
[Butterflies]

Beautiful, Flitting
Shining in the sun
Golden, Vibrant
'Til the day is done

Dipping, Swirling
Spreading pollen all around
Once a little caterpillar
Crawling on the ground

~*~

Mariposas is more than a poem about butterflies. It is a metaphor about my life. I was lost in a world of depression and felt like I was that caterpillar, crawling around on the ground, confused and all alone. But in the last year and a half I have found a new hope in my renewed relationship with my Lord and Savior, Jesus Christ. He has lifted me out of the depths of my depression. I have gone back to work fulltime after a nine-year hiatus from reality due to the depression I lived within. I have become a valuable part of society once again. I speak in my Church part time and am looking forward to one day working in the ministry full time. I, like the caterpillar, have found my wing and I am soaring higher than before. For my wings are the Everlasting Arms of Jesus!
Nov 3, 2003

~*~

As I type this it is almost two years later and Jesus is still my Wings in the wind and I soar even higher that I did before. I was Ordained into ministry by my church, Bread of Life Christian Fellowship, Mound House, Nevada in March of this year. Thank You Lord for the freedom You have given me.
Oct 08, 2005

Mariposas

A Living Sacrifice

Jesus, You called us to give ourselves as a living, breathing
sacrifice. Here I am laid out on my bed, much as the sacrificial
lambs were laid out on the altar in days of old. This is my
sacrifice to You. Take my life, all that I am, all that I could be.
All of my hopes, dreams and desires. I give them to You right
now and forever. Use me as You choose. Send me where You
would have me to go. To do ALL that You have for me to do.
Now and forever; I AM YOURS! This is my reasonable
sacrifice. And I offer it to You for all eternity. Amen

~*~

"I beseech you therefore, brethren, by
the mercies of God, that ye present your
bodies a living sacrifice, holy, acceptable
to God, which is your reasonable service."
Romans 12:1

FAITH

I have Faith yet doubt remains
Free me from it's recurring chains

It claims my mind without a thought
About the answer YOUR love has bought

And there YOU sit and wait for me
The calm within this doubtful sea

Thank YOU for the peace YOU bring
I know YOU are my conquering KING

~*~

Jesus said unto him, if thou canst believe,
all things are possible unto him that
believeth. And straightway the father of
the child cried out, and said with tears,
Lord I believe; help Thou my unbelief.
Mark 9:23-24

~*~

And when Jesus was entered into Capernaum, there came unto him a
centurion, beseeching him, and saying, Lord, my servant lieth at home
sick of the palsy, grievously tormented. And Jesus saith unto him, I
will come and heal him. The centurion answered and said, Lord, I am
not worthy that thou shouldest come under my roof: but speak the
word only, and my servant shall be healed. For I am a man under
authority, having soldiers under me: and I say to this man, Go, and he
goeth; and to another, come, and he cometh; and to my servant, Do
this, and he doeth it. When Jesus heard it, he marveled, and said to
them that followed, Verily I say unto you, I have not found so great
faith, no, not in Israel. Matthew 8:5-10

Nothing is Free!

A very costly FREE GIFT, this is what my Salvation is
to me. You gave it to me freely. I accept it and receive
it freely, too. Yet it COST You *everything*! You set aside
Your glory and majesty to put on humanity like a royal
robe. You walked among us that we might learn to follow
You. And You died the most cruel death imaginable
upon the cross, giving up Your physical life that we may
find Life Eternal. Thank You, Lord, for this wonderful
gift that You gave so freely. This Grace. This gift of
True Life, Everlasting, IN YOU!

~*~

"For by grace ye are saved through faith;
And that not of yourselves: it is the gift of
God: not of works, lest any man should boast."
Ephesians 2:8-9

Setting Goals

What is the destination we seek?
Is it a heavenly palace, or a precipice steep?
Money and wealth or a place at His feet
Whatever your goals, the beginning you see
Is where you must choose the right path for thee
Too often we find as we travel the road
That the path isn't leading to our intended goal
The wide, lovely path often ends in despair
So choosing your road must be done with great care
Let Jesus guide you, from beginning to end
He never will leave you; He's your faithful friend
The way is not easy, but His path is best
As you climb to the high places you'll master each test
For the end of life's journey is His Kingdom and Rest!

~*~

He hath shewed thee, oh man, what is
good, and what doth the Lord require of
thee, but to do justly, and to love mercy,
and to walk humbly with your God.
Micah 6:8

~*~

And whosoever doth not bear his cross, and come after me, cannot be
my disciple. For which of you, intending to build a tower, sitteth not
down first, and counteth the cost, whether he have sufficient to finish
it? Lest haply, after he hath laid the foundation, and is not able to
finish it, all that behold it begin to mock him, Luke 14:27-29

Free to Forgive

Forgiveness is so important to our lives. The lack of it cripples us and our walk with God. It also hinders our relationship with the person we are harboring this unforgiveness against. And it will stifle their walk with God as much or more than it hurts our own. It wraps them in a bondage as strong as prison chains.

~*~

Lord, hear my cry. Cleanse my heart from sin; especially this one. If I am harboring unforgiveness against any of your creations, please show me where and how to truly forgive. My prayers of repentance set them free to love, serve and worship You. And free me from it's chains, too. In Jesus Name, amen.

~*~

Judge not, and ye shall not be judged: condemn not, and ye shall not be condemned: forgive and ye shall be forgiven: give and it shall be given unto you; good measure, pressed down, and shaken together, and running over, shall men give into your bosom. For with the measure ye mete withal it shall be measured to you again. Luke 6:37, 38

Answered Prayer

God <u>always</u> answers <u>all</u> our prayers.
We may not always receive what we ask for.
Or it may not come right when we ask. For
"Yes" is not always the best answer for us.
 God, like our earthly parents, only wants
to give us good gifts. So He may say, "Yes."
Or He may say, "No." Or He may say,
"Wait on Me and I will give it to you at the
right time."

~*~

And whatever things you ask in prayer,
Believing, you will receive.
Matt 21:22,NIV

This verse says we will receive, but it doesn't say when!

~*~

Every good and every perfect gift is from
above and comes down from the Father of Lights.
James 1:17, NKJV

~*~

God does answer Every Prayer,
Every Time and With the BEST
Possible answer for us, Always!

In His Image

God is not walking the earth in a physical
body at this time. Yet Christians are called
'the body of Christ.' If we are full of His
love in our hearts we will be perfected -
completed and mature – in Him. Then we
will have His likeness in us; He will truly
be visible in our lives. When we are so
full of His love that we begin to take on
more of His likeness we should be pouring
that love out on those around us. Sharing His
love so that they will want to be more like
Him too.

~*~

No man hath seen God at any time.
If we love one another, God dwelleth
in us, and His love is perfected in us.
I John 4:12

~*~

Lord, You are love in its purest form.
Fill me up to overflowing with Your love
that I may pour You out on all those
around me. May my love be pure and
holy as You are. Amen!

Guilt No More

Guilt is not in Your hands
Righteousness and mercy
Are at Your command

Satan would fill us with guilty refrain
But all this must flea
When we call on Your name

And call we shall do, each and every day
As we walk in Your grace
And follow Your way

At the cross You did free us from guilt's spin
And when this life's over
ALL will see that You win!

~*~

My dear children, let's not just talk about love; let's practice
real love. This is the only way we'll know we're living truly,
living in God's reality. It's also the way to shut down
debilitating self-criticism, even when there is something to it.
For God is greater than our worried hearts and knows more
about us than we do ourselves. I John 3:18-20 NIV

All Things

I can do all things through Christ who strengthens me
I can do all things through Christ who delivers me
Through Christ alone, Through Christ alone

He calms all my fears and He dries all my tears,
He restores all the years that have flown.
He alone is the one; He completes what He's begun
when you take Him as your own.

I can do all things through Christ who strengthens me
I can do all things through Christ who delivers me
Through Christ alone, Through Christ alone

Jesus Christ is the One; He is God's Only Son.
He can save you and make you whole.
He will heal you heart; and His wisdom He'll impart.
And He'll dwell with you deep in your soul.

Then you can do all things through Christ who strengthens you
You can do all things through Christ who delivers you
Through Christ alone, Through Christ alone

We can do all things through Christ who strengthens us
We can do all things through Christ who delivers us
Through Christ alone, Through Christ alone

~*~

I can do all things through Christ which
strengtheneth me. Philippians 4:13

~*~

I know I can do all things You put before me, Lord. As You are my
strength. Keep me strong, Dear Lord. Fill me with Your mighty
power. And keep me on task. Let me not stray from the things You
would have me to do, or the path You have chosen for me to walk.
Some days it is just so hard. I get tired and run down. But then I call
on You, and you pick me up again. You infuse my body with Your
strength. You sustain me. I am so blessed to have such a wonderfully
loving and caring Father. Thank You Lord!

P R A Y E R

Pouring out our hearts to God
Requesting Him to hear and answer
Awaiting, in patience, His reply
Yes is NOT always the right answer
Expecting He knows what is best
Receiving from Him and walking it out in faith

~*~

Thank You Lord, for listening!

~*~

And the prayer of faith shall save the sick,
and the Lord shall raise him up; and if he
have committed sins, they shall be forgiven
him. Confess your faults one to another,
and pray one for another, that ye may be
healed. The effectual fervent prayer of a
righteous man availeth much. James 5:15, 16

Nearer

Draw me ever nearer, Lord
Through the stormy blast
Though trial and tear assail me
They will never last

For life's earthly battles
Shall soon all be past
Forever to be standing
In your presence Lord, at last

~*~

For, lo, they that are far from thee shall perish:
thou hast destroyed all them that go a whoring
from thee. But it is good for me to draw near
to God: I have put my trust in the Lord GOD,
that I may declare all thy works.
Psalm 72:27-28

Vessels of the Lord

We are all the Lord's vessels in various
stages of completion. There are even
times when we need to be "re-thrown" on
the Potter's Wheel to repair the
imperfections that have shown through
from life's trials. And some times, Lord,
You have to break us because the firing
process has caused impurities to come to
the surface. You throw us into the clay
bin add a bit of Your Water of Life to
wash us clean. Then You will place us on
You wheel again to be remade into a
vessel of honor for your Kingdom. When
we pass through that firing for the last
time we are finally perfected. Gilded for
the Kings table to shine bright for all
eternity. How wonderful to be a vessel of
Honor for Your Glory!

~*~

But now, O LORD, thou art our father; we are the clay, and thou our
potter; and we all are the work of thy hand.
Isaiah 64:8

Nay but, O man, who art thou that repliest against God? Shall the
thing formed say to him that formed it,
Why hast thou made me thus? Hath not the potter power over the
clay, of the same lump to make one vessel unto honor, and another
unto dishonor? What if God, willing to shew his wrath, and to make
his power known, endured with much longsuffering the vessels of
wrath fitted to destruction: And that he might make known the riches
of his glory on the vessels of mercy, which he had afore prepared unto
glory, Even us, whom he hath called, not of the Jews only, but also of
the Gentiles? Romans 9:20-24

That Good Part

Oh to sit at Jesus' feet
Listening to his words so sweet
Constantly abiding there
With not a worry nor a care!

~*~

Now it came to pass, as they went, that he entered into a certain village: and a certain woman named Martha received him into her house. And she had a sister called Mary, which also sat at Jesus' feet, and heard his word. But Martha was cumbered about much serving, and came to him, and said, Lord, dost thou not care that my sister hath left me to serve alone? Bid her therefore that she help me. And Jesus answered and said unto her; Martha, Martha, thou art careful and troubled about many things: But one thing is needful: and Mary has chosen *that good part*, which shall not be taken away from her.
Luke 10:38-42

~*~

As I sit here resting this afternoon, I feel more Mary like than usual. I find myself constantly living in the tyranny of the urgent, running from one task to another from dawn to dark. But these last few days I have not been able to run to and fro as I am healing from a recent surgery. So I have been working on some much needed writing and in the process listening to various Christian teachers on our local radio station. God had to put me in this place so that I could appreciate the Mary side of me before I must be a Martha again. We each need to take time to appreciate our Mary side, for we all live too much as a Martha. With all of our technology we have become a micro-minute society – we want everything and we want it in 30 seconds or less. This hurry-up mentality isn't all bad, but it isn't all good either. It just leaves us with a longing that we tend not to realize we have. That longing is for a more peaceful pace - for the Mary side of life - just sitting at Jesus feet.

That Good Part

Living Stones

As steel sharpens steel, and a diamond
can only be cut by another diamond, so
the Lord Jesus uses others in our lives to
trim away our rough edges and make us
into that RARE and PRECIOUS gem for
His crowning glory that He ALWAYS
knew we would be.

Thank You, Lord!

~*~

"Ye also, as lively stones, are built up a
spiritual house, an holy priesthood, to
offer up spiritual sacrifices, acceptable to
God by Jesus Christ."
1 Peter 2:5

Is Your Mess Awful, Or AWE-Full

I asked myself this question today as I
was in my 'quiet time.' As humans we
tend to have messes of the awful variety.
Yet as followers of Jesus, He can turn
awful into AWE-full, just like He did in
the garden tomb all those years ago.

Death thought he had beaten the Lord of
Life, but he was mistaken. Jesus gave his
body over to death for three days and
nights. But on that fourth morning Jesus
breathed the breath of Life anew.

If Jesus can conquer death, He can turn
even our most awful situation into
something truly AWE-full. I know this,
because He took the life of this love starved,
lonely addict and brought her Life, Love, and
Hope for a Real future as a woman full of
Him. His Love. His Life. Ever living to
proclaim His truth everyday and everywhere.

Is your mess awful?
Let Jesus make it AWE-full!

~*~

Whether therefore ye eat, or drink,
or whatsoever ye do, do all to the
glory of God. 1 Corinthians 10:31

Facing the Giants

Giants falling all around
No army is in sight
Just a shepherd boy standing there
God's Spirit is his might
Not trusting in his strength alone
But taking God's as his own
Felling life's giants one by one
The other giants start to run
For God fights on his side

~*~

The battle belongs to the Lord!

~*~

"It is not by sword or spear that the Lord saves; for the battle is the Lord's, and He will give all of you into our hands."
1 Samuel 17:47 NIV

~*~

Then said David to the Philistine, Thou comest to me with a sword, and with a spear, and with a shield: but I come to thee in the name of the LORD of hosts, the God of the armies of Israel, whom thou hast defied. This day will the LORD deliver thee into mine hand; and I will smite thee, and take thine head from thee ... And David put his hand in his bag, and took thence a stone, and slang it, and smote the Philistine in his forehead, that the stone sunk into his forehead; and he fell upon his face to the earth. So David prevailed over the Philistine with a sling and with a stone, and smote the Philistine, and slew him... 1 Samuel 17:45, 46a, 49, 50a.

Facing the Giants

Mountains in our Lives

The Mountains in our lives
May not be rock and dirt
But memories of our brokenness
The sorrow and the hurt

Jesus died on Calvary
These Mountains to remove
And lift us into His Throne Room
His faithful Love to prove

~*~

Thank You, Lord
For removing the mountains in my life
And giving me the Faith To believe that You could.
Please keep up the Shovel Brigade!

~*~

Jesus replied, "I tell you the truth, if you
have faith and do not doubt, not only can
you do what was done to the fig tree, but
also you can say to this mountain, 'Go,
throw yourself into the sea,' and it will be
done." Matthew 21:21

Remaining in the Light

As soon as we realize the blessings God has given us, Satan comes right in to throw rocks at our spiritual light to plunge us into darkness again. He doesn't want us to see the light or feel the joy and freedom it brings us. It is his job to keep us plodding along in our darkness and suffering.

But the light of Life is far greater. All we have to do is stay connected. Our salvation connects us to this light. We stay connected by building our faith each day. And faith is built by "hearing" the Word.

By reading the Bible we also begin the renewing of our minds. We change our thought patterns to those He would have us to think, as in our example of Philippians 4:8.

Also by accepting His joy and peace – in spite of how things look or how we "feel." We can guard our light by knowing and wearing God's armor, Ephesians 6:10-20.

So let's gear up for the fight. It is at times both a spiritual and physical battle. I John 1:5 & 7 NIV says 'God is light and in Him is no darkness at all. . .But if we walk in the Light as he is in the Light, we have fellowship with one another.'

Staying in fellowship with other believers is part of building our faith for they can lift us up in their prayers when the battle is fierce. And we can do likewise for them in their need.

We all have strengths and weaknesses, which God uses to compliment one another. My strength may be an area in which you are weak, so you could lean on me for strength in that area. Likewise your strength may be my weakness, so I can help you through your time of need. And we can both walk on in the Light of His Love together, strengthening each other along the way.

Thank you, Lord for the fellowship of like-minded believers!

All Hallows Eve?

While looking toward the days ahead
I feel unusually drawn
To focus on the things of God
And of the glory to come

Yet today as I sit and muse
There are those who say
The holiday at this week's end
Is a wonderful, glorious day

I fear that they are unaware
Of the wicked start the holiday had
Of the giving of gifts to the dead
Or the deeds done that were bad

"Trick or Treat" should not be
Taken lightly by folks
For in days of old the Celts and Druids
Did such sinister "jokes"

When on this day of the year
The folk would lay out food
To appease the spirits of the dead
And save their foul mood

It has been told of former days
The "spirits" did commit
Acts of violence and of rage
On those whose gifts they didn't get

Fires burned, homes and crops destroyed
When folk the dead did neglect
For those of the local cults did rage
When these spirit's needs were not met

I know that times have changed
And folk have long forgot
The origins of this 'holy' day

So these things are not taught
But we do well to teach these truths
Before our kids go out
To plunder the city for candy sweet
And "Trick or Treat" do shout

Remembering the days of old
Our forefathers did honor thus
Redeem the time that Satan stole
Giving praise to God A MUST

A party in honor of our King
Is a much more glorious way
To redeem the day that Satan stole
And is using to steal our children away

Our church has chosen a fitting way
To honor God and thus our children protect
Creation Celebration is
Our church's fall project

So "chose today whom you shall serve"
And give your heart to honor all He's given
And remember that heaven is a place
Reserved only for the living!

Beware, The Evil One

The love of God it never changes
It stays the same from day to day
Though what we value rearranges
His perfect love will never stray

When Satan always is deceiving
If we to Christ would go
Then what our hearts are firm believing
He can in no way stow

Yet if our heart begins to falter
The enemy floods in
And steals our heart from the altar
And leads away our soul to sin

No, Satan can't from His love take us
When we fully follow God
But if we his lies start believing
Then from God's chosen path we'll trod

~*~

Neither death, nor life, nor angels, nor principalities, nor
powers, nor things present, nor things to come, nor height,
nor depth, nor any other creature, shall be able to separate
us from the love of God, which is in Christ Jesus our Lord.
Romans 8:38-39

In the Midst of Trouble

In the midst of our greatest trouble we are <u>never alone</u>. You stand with us and walk beside us all the way. It is a wonderful blessing to know we never have to face these trials all alone. For You have said, "I will never leave thee, nor forsake thee." Thank You, Lord, for this great and wonderful promise.

~*~

"Though I walk in the midst of trouble, thou wilt revive me: thou shalt stretch forth thine hand against the wrath of mine enemies, and thy right hand shall save me." Psalm 138:7 KJV

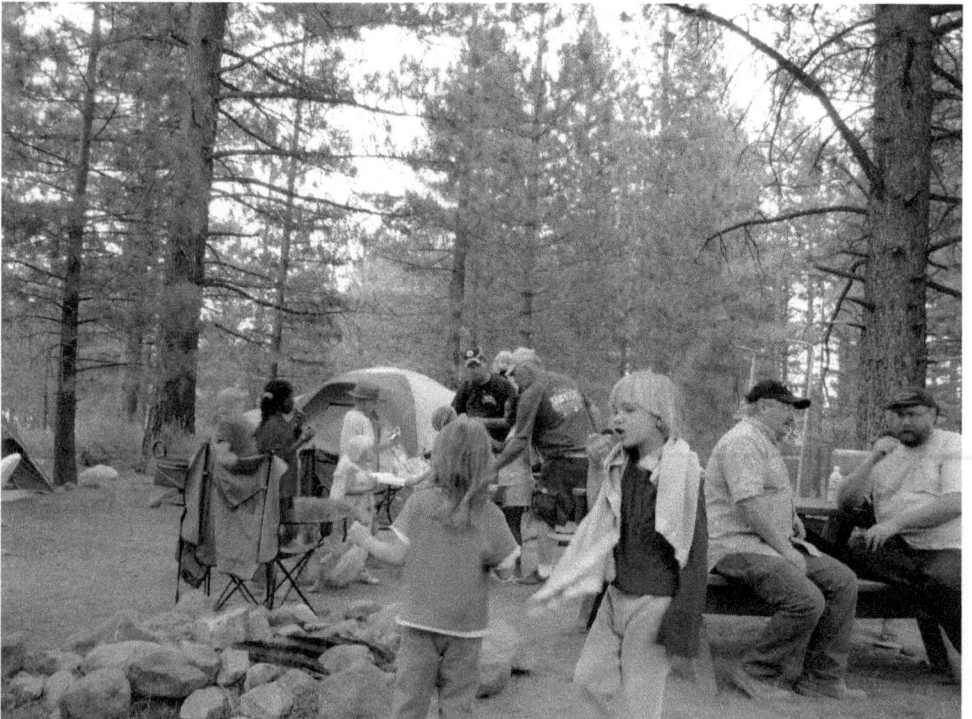

Praising Him

Wonderful songs of praise I sing
Extolling the glory of my King
Worshiping thus my heart renews
Blessing me down into my shoes
Freeing me from care, stress and pain
Reviving my spirit once again
Humbly at Your feet I lay
All the cares of many a past day
Refreshed, renewed, revived once more
Ready to walk through the open church door
Back into the world at hand
Obediently to follow Your every command
Sharing Your word with others I do
That they also may learn to follow You
And when I feel that my strength is gone
And I can no longer carry on
I wait for the day, 'tis coming soon
When I can forever sing Your glorious tunes
To again be refreshed, renewed, restored
There in the presence of my King, my Lord

~*~

The Spirit of the Lord GOD is upon me;
because the LORD hath anointed me ...
To appoint unto them that mourn in
Zion, to give unto them beauty for ashes,
the oil of joy for mourning, the garment
of praise for the spirit of heaviness; that
they may be called the trees of
righteousness, the planting of the Lord,
that He might be glorified. Isaiah 61: 1a, 3

Lost Sheep

I was born in the fold as a wobbly lamb
Contented to be fed by the Shepherds own hand
One day I learned of the world beyond
Suddenly all my contentment was gone
New things to hear, new sights to see
I had to get out there to see what they be
I wandered away from the safety I'd known
The Shepherd, the fold, the other sheep that He owned
I found a new flock, what a scraggly bunch
So I walked in among them to partake of their lunch
Wild grasses abundant and weeds galore
I feasted and feasted, but still wanted more
Wild grasses taste sweeter, but they don't satisfy
So I wandered off eating whatever caught my eye
My wool got all dirty, filled with thorns and twigs
But I had my freedom; I didn't give a fig
Till finally I noticed I was cold and alone
The new flock was gone. I was all on my own
Far from my family, my Shepherd and home
Crying and scared, lying in a dark cave
My Shepherd came looking His lost one to save
Back to the sheep fold, my family and friends
The Shepherd did take me and feed me again
He combed out my wool and gave me a bath
Now I was contented, truly satisfied, At Last!
Forever I'll stay with the Shepherd to abide
Happy, contented, and fully satisfied!

~*~

Let my soul live, and it shall praise thee; and let thy
judgments help me. I have gone astray like a lost
sheep; seek thy servant; for I do not forget thy
commandments. Psalm 119:175-176

Waiting on the Lord

What is waiting on the Lord? I believe it is more than mere anticipation. It is a joyful, trusting and an expectant, anticipating.

Knowing that the Lord only gives good gifts to His children. And trusting He alone knows what is best for
each one of us. Then waiting expectantly, like a family expecting their first child, for the Lord to bless us.

But waiting is also serving the Lord God with every fiber of our being; body, soul, mind and spirit.

Faithfully <u>doing</u> all we do as unto the Lord. Whether it be acts of ministry for and to others, sharing a meal with a needy family, or cleaning the bathroom in your home or your house of worship, it can all be an act of waiting on our Lord.

~*~

Therefore "wait" I say, on the Lord
with all of your might!

~*~

But they that wait upon the Lord shall renew their strength; they shall mount up with wings as eagles; they shall run, and not be weary; and they shall walk, and not faint. Isaiah 40:31

Working for the Master
(An Ode to Lovely Feet)

Give your best unto the Master
Shine His Light to all you meet
Without Him life would be disaster
We would not have "lovely feet"

All of life should be collecting
Lives we've brought unto the king
It should also be reflecting
Changes He to us did bring

Are you sharing Him with others
In the words your mouth does speak?
This is how we build the Kingdom
How we're blessed with "lovely feet"

Share His love with friends and neighbors
Rightly speak His words of truth
Be not ashamed to share His message
Whether to aged one or youth

Give your best unto the Master
Shine His Light to all you meet
Help them avoid life's grave disaster
Then you will have "lovely feet"

~*~

How lovely on the mountains are the feet of him who brings Good
News, who announces peace and brings Good News of happiness, who
announces Salvation, and says unto Zion, Your God reigns!
Isaiah 57:7 NASB

The Good News is the Gospel Message!

~*~

"Study to shew thyself approved unto God, a workman that needeth
not to be ashamed, rightly dividing the word of truth." II Tim. 2:15,
KJV

SUPPLICATIONS

Spending time
Upon your knees
Praying to the Lord
Pleading for an answer clear
Longing for a word
Intently seeking Jesus' face
Crying from your heart
Awaiting His precious touch of grace
Trusting He will impart
Indued with His Spirit
Onward down the road to trod
Never willing to leave His presence
Staying in tune with the will of God

~*~

Be careful for nothing; but in everything by prayer and supplication with thanksgiving let your requests be made known to God.
Philippians 4:6

Empty or Full?

Empty we come into this life. And if we seek a life of rewards for their own sake, to fill our "trophy case", we will leave it in the very same way.

Empty of a relationship with Jesus, who created us for this express purpose. Empty of the things that bring real meaning to our lives; Worshiping and Serving Him. Empty of true Love; for Jesus is that Love. And Empty of the rewards He gives to us for a life of dedication and devotion to Him. The rewards He has to offer are more valuable than any earthly riches can buy. For to me, the greatest reward He could ever give is a very simple phrase spoken in His Love; "Well done, My child, well done!"

So I encourage, no challenge I you to seek to be Full! Full of His presence. Full of His Love, Peace and Joy. Full of the Gifts of His Spirit as listed in Galatians 5:22-26. Full of the Wisdom that only comes from following close to Him and daily seeking His face.

~*~

"The thief comes only to steal and kill and destroy; I have come that they may have life, and have it to the Full."
John 10:10 NIV

Rain

It seems to bring much darkness
As it hovers o're the land
And yet it brings refreshing
To the barren, desert sand
It is the same in Jesus
When shadows o're us roll
For when the darkness leaves us
There is joy within our soul

On earth the rain brings flowers
To bloom along our way
From heaven, it God's blessings
That will brighten up our day
And though we may not choose
The rain-darkened path
It is the Light of Jesus love
Which doth conquer it at last

~*~

Nevertheless He left not Himself without
witness, in that He did good, and gave us
rain from heaven, and fruitful seasons,
filling our hearts with food and gladness.
Acts 14:17

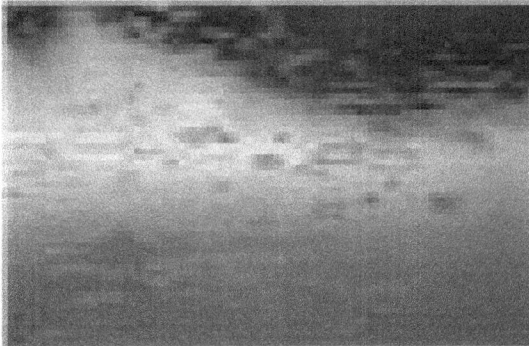

Blessed

Why are we so blessed?
Because He loved us so
Why so full of happiness?
He chose to save our souls

So He gave His life
To ransom me from sin
What a wonderful pardon
What a joy to be clean

Blessings all Eternal
From Abraham's Seed
Upon us freely poured out
And now we are freed

From a life full of bondage
From our sin and distress
To a life full of His riches
Thus we are bountifully blessed!

~*~

Blessed are the pure in heart:
for they shall see God!
Matthew 5:8

A Tree in God's Garden

And he shall be like a tree planted by the
rivers of water, that bringeth forth his fruit in
his season; his leaf shall not wither; and
whatsoever he doeth shall prosper. Psalm 1:3

~*~

Each of our lives is symbolic of this tree.
If we are rooted and grounded in Jesus
and His Holy Word. Watered by His
springs of living water – the Holy Spirit –
our fruit shall be plenteous and sweet.

We should cultivate the Word. Dig into it
deeply. Have you ever seen a picture of a
lush, beautiful tree in the middle of a vast
desert? Huge and green by comparison?
The land all around may look dry and
barren, but the River of Life runs deep
beneath the surface. That tree has sunk
it's life giving roots deep into it's ground
and found the flow within the heart of the
earth. It doesn't allow the natural landscape
to keep it from living and growing strong
and beautiful.

Ignore your circumstances, like this desert tree.
And plant your roots deep in the Word of God.
Spread your "branches" in praise to Jesus. Send
your roots in to the depths of His marvelous
"Springs of Living Water." Be fruitful and Grow
Strong in HIM!

A Tree in God's Garden

Real Sight

Clearly do I see all you have done for me
Blind was I before, but now I truly see
Darkness filled my life, no light was found within
I was buried in despair by my multitude of sin
Somehow You broke through all the darkness in my life
You freed me from its chains and rid me of it's strife
Blind was I before, but now I truly see
Your love broke through and set this captive free
Imprisoned by the debt of sin, this weight upon my soul
You reached down from Calvary and truly made me whole
How blind I was to life and love, but now I clearly see
With but a drop of Your precious blood, indeed I am set free
Today I share with others Your love that set me free
And how I did in darkness live, but Now I truly see

Thank You, Lord for saving me!

~*~

Through these he has given us his very great and precious promises, so that through them you may participate in the divine nature and escape the corruption in the world caused by evil desires. For this very reason, make every effort to add to your faith goodness; and to goodness, knowledge; and to knowledge, self-control; and to self-control, perseverance; and to perseverance, godliness; and to godliness, brotherly kindness; and to brotherly kindness, love. For if you possess these qualities in increasing measure, they will keep you from being ineffective and unproductive in your knowledge of our Lord Jesus Christ. But if anyone does not have them, he is nearsighted and blind, and has forgotten that he has been cleansed from his past sins. 1 Peter 1:4-9

For he who lacks these things is shortsighted, even to blindness, and has forgotten that he was cleansed from his old sins. 2 Peter 1:9

Abundant Life!

Is there anything sweeter than a new life
full of meaning and purpose? Once I was
lost, a drift in the world like a ship
without a compass to plot my coarse. It
was dark and life wasn't worth living. I
tried many times to end it, but He knew
better. He found me in that bottomless
pit and filled me with the light of His
presence, and a new, abundant life.

Now it thrills my soul beyond measure to
share this new life with others. Jesus is
why my life now has meaning. I can, will,
and do pass His message on to others who
are as lost in their darkness as I once was.
To share this abundant life I have found in
Jesus.

~*~

All that ever came before me are thieves and robbers:
but the sheep did not hear them. I am the door: by me
if any man enter in, he shall be saved, and shall go in
and out, and find pasture. The thief cometh not, but for
to steal, and to kill, and to destroy: *I am come that they
might have life, and that they might have it more abundantly.*
John 10:8-10

Richness

Are you filled with Love unending?
Is there deep compassion there?
Or is self the ruler of your heart?
Sitting boldly on its chair?

Self can not true richness bring
Even if there's gold for all
For he is a shallow king
And quickly leads to a great fall

When Christ is Master of your life
And He makes your heart His home
He can real riches bring
As he rules from your life's throne

Making clean your hidden places
He fills you with His Love inside
Spread His Love around to others
While walking closely to His side

As you share the Gospel story
Your heart's treasures will grow and grow
For it matters not if you have money
But only the riches He will bestow!

~*~

Richness is not counted by the wealth we have gained.
True richness is proven in each person by the spirit,
Holy or unholy, that dwells within.

~*~

"Rich and poor meet together: the Lord
is the maker of them ALL."
Proverbs 22:2

The Old, Sweet Rose Bush

Many have been the battles of my life; some of my own making due to wrong choices. Others due to the trials and testing of this life I have hidden in Christ. But no matter their source; all have taught me valuable lessons that have encouraged me to minister to those Jesus has placed in my life.

Each time I have been broken, battered, and bruised has only made me stronger in my person and my faith. Jesus has never given up on me.

All of this reminds me of the old rose bush in my front yard that has weathered many storms in its life. This spring a couple of young men repainted my house. This rose bush was growing up against the building, wrapping itself around the corner of the house. In preparing the house for painting they had to pull the bush away from the house it had leaned on for many years. In this they broke it's main branch.

When I arrived home that evening they showed me the damage and asked if it could be repaired. I asked them if they had a roll of duct tape. They got the tape for me and I tapped it together and tied it to another tree for support.

This repair job took place a couple of months ago. The rose bush is still alive and now is covered with beautiful pink roses.

Jesus has done this type of binding up and repair on my life many times. He has bound up my broken heart and limbs and made me to bear beautiful fruit to His glory.

Thank you Lord!

WHO AM I?

When I look into my mirror
Who do I see?
I do not know the person
Looking back at me
She is a foreign object
Of curious design
I do not recognize her,
Is that face really mine?
Then the voice of Jesus
Whispers in my ear
This is my beautiful daughter
And you should have no fear
A new creation in ME
You have finally become
The old lady is now dead
The new you is now come
In the furnace of purity
I have placed you for a while
To make of you a sparkling gem
My bright and shinning child
There will be rough times
In the days ahead
But when the road is bumpy
By MY hand you will be lead
Don't judge thing by appearance
Use MY eyes as your guide
For you see the outside
I while I look from inside
I know things are confusing
You don't know where to go
Be still my little daughter
And take things very slow
I am grooming you for the Kingdom
A rare and precious PEARL
You will never be who you once were
But you will always be My girl

You have a bright tomorrow
It's hidden in My hand
And when the time is perfect
Before you it will stand
I wish to keep it secret
So you will be surprised
I can hardly wait to show you
And see the tears of joy in your eyes
It is not meant to punish you
That the process takes so long
It is to build your character
And make your spirit strong
So wait a little longer
And soon you will see
The lady I have made of you
A real PEARL you shall be
So when you look in the mirror
Don't try your face to see
Look well beyond surface
To see My face in thee
And when next time you question
The promises I've made
You will have the answers
Upon your heart they're laid
I only keep a secret
Until the time is right
For I wish you to jump for joy
And sing praises of delight
I know your heart is lonely
So come and sit with Me
We'll talk about the universe
And all eternity
And IF the day should happen
That you should find a spouse
He will be whom I've chosen
For you to keep his house
For each day comes a lesson
To teach you help-meet chores
And also to help him become
The man that's perfectly yours

For when I do the choosing
You two, a perfect match will be
It will be worth all your waiting
Just be patient child, and see

04/07/2008

A Sweeter Life?

Sitting on a rock
I found a hollow spot
A dark and lonely tomb
It has all kinds of room
One could get lost therein

I reached my hand inside
The room was deep and wide
To swallow me was the goal
For then it could steal my soul
And I would be lost again

On the edge I teeter
I wanted a life much sweeter
So I heard a lie instead
It told how I might get ahead
But only if I listen

I wanted to believe
That sweet life to receive
And so I started to wander in
But it was dark with sin
Could I see the Son from within?

Sickly I became
Wounded, bruised and lame
Sweeter life did not become
How could I ever be so dumb
That clear voice to hearken?

So from the dark I cried
With the Son I want to abide
He heard my voice and came
And rescued me from shame
TO Him I only want to listen

He cleared my shattered mind
Said my sins where all behind
He bound up my wounded parts
And put His song back in my heart
I know I am now whole once again

I'll ALWAYS sing His praise
And worship Him all my days
I'll not seek the "easy road"
To try to lighten my OWN load
But lay on Him my heavy burden

Are you sitting on a rock?
Staring at that dark spot?
Do you long for a life more sweet?
Looking for a more comfortable seat?
Do you teeter on the edge while looking in?

Let me tell you my friend
The sweeter life's not therein
Only sin and death you'll find
And a cloud overcomes your mind
If you choose that strange voice to hearken

It may sound sure and true
But you'll end up in bondage, too
Listen to my warning call
And don't follow strangers at all
For dark and gloomy is that place within

If you on that edge do teeter
And you hope for something sweeter
Turn around, on Jesus call
He will keep you from that fall
And fill you with songs of praises deep within

Listen only to the Master
Any other leads to disaster
Safety reigns within His fold
And when you're scared, you He will hold
And calm your troubled spirit once again

Now that I have warned you clearly
And the Master seems more dearly
Share this tale with those nearby
Hope to quell their anguished cry
And keep them from falling into sin

If we all do our part
We may save some tender heart
Help them not to go astray
And with bumps and bruises pay
We may keep them from falling into sin

Protect your neighbor and your friend
It will reward you in the end
Help them stay on the right road
And maybe lighten their heavy load
Giving Glory unto Jesus unto the end

9-11 & 9/12 2008

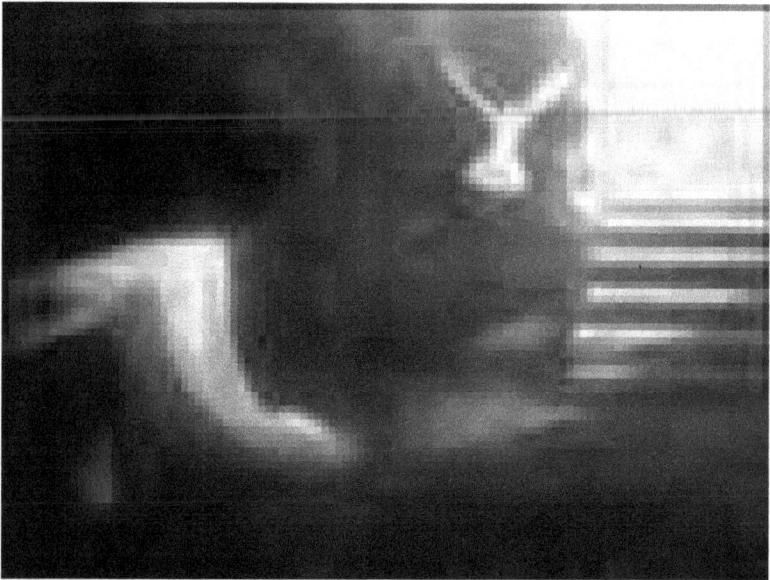

The Lonely Sparrow

Like a lonely, little sparrow atop the house I sit
Dwelling on Jesus every little bit

Waiting for another to come and share my view
Though the longed for visits are often very few

This solitary lifestyle may seem empty to you
But Jesus ever sits beside me to share my peaceful view

His praises I will sing forever from my lofty perch
Whether or not He sends another to share my little verse

For loneliness can't dwell within when Jesus fills the soul
For sharing Him with others is to be the only goal

So here atop the house I sit and sing the gospel song
And Jesus ever shares my time while drawing others to sing along

~*~

I watch, and I am as a sparrow
alone upon the house top.
Psalm 102:7

Freedom

When the world crowds in
And you're tempted to sin
Find the friend close at hand
And vent from within
Give yourself freedom to release
And be in sweet peace
Your friend can be true
Lending a hand to you
And lead you to Jesus feet

When your circumstances change
And you have joy in place of rage
Give your friend a big hug
Do not be afraid – she's no bug
Perhaps she'll need your help one day
Be willing to share
Or to just lend an ear
And give her the freedom she needs
Together with Jesus you'll meet.

A freedom to vent
And then to repent
What a blessed part of friendship, indeed!

PEARLS

Pure and
Exciting, but
Always a
Real
Lady.

Again, the kingdom of heaven is like unto a merchant man, seeking goodly pearls: Who, when He had found one pearl of great price, went and sold all that he had, and bought it. Matthew 13:45-46

~*~

We are the PEARLS Jesus is seeking!

Still Single

God gave a single lifestyle to me
He gave no ending date
If He should choose to tarry
Then I will gladly wait

When friends and loved ones marry
I will not hang my head
I will dance at every wedding
Thus worshipping God instead

God alone knows the best way
The path each one should take
He has given me much ministry
To many lives that are at stake

Being single gives me space
To serve Him every day
My only obligation
Is to trust Him and Obey

I love to work for Jesus
To fulfill His every call
But if I had a family
From this pathway I might fall

I would like a human husband
Some one with whom to talk
But my Heavenly Husband
Has chosen the road that I should walk

I serve my Lord with gladness
And will do so all my life
Even if I have no husband
No one to call me wife

For Jesus is my provider
He supplies my every need
There is no greater husband
Than He who died for me

If you find yourself living single
In this there is no disgrace
For Jesus has called you to it
And filled you with His grace
Make the Lord your Heavenly Husband
And heed His ministry call
Singleness gives you the freedom
To be the servant of all

So serve the Lord with gladness
As you gaze upon His face
And thank Him for His precious gifts
Of His singleness and His grace

Leigh
6/30/09

Kissed By The Beloved

Have you been held by the Beloved
Caressed lovingly by His hands
Wrapped up in the love He offers
Held close and listening for His commands
Jesus longs to closely hold you
Gently to caress you with His love
To share with you His deepest secrets
All the things for you He's planned

Have you been betrothed to the Beloved
Waiting for your joining to be complete
Are you ever listening for His closeness
Sitting daily at His feet
Jesus longs for you to join Him
Wants you as His loving Bride
Seeks to seat you at His table
In the place of Honor, by His side

Have you been kissed by the Beloved
Joined in oneness, wed to Him
Have you left behind all darkness
And your former life of sin
Jesus longs to kiss you deeply
Waits to see you long the same
See Him standing in the pathway
He longs to take all guilt and pain

Were are you, oh bride of Jesus
Are you longing to know more of Him
Have you shunned all the world's dainties
For the Best of Heaven to win
Shed your former lifestyle
Leave the past all behind
Seek the kisses of the Beloved
Seek His very heart to find

I've been kissed by the Beloved
I've been held close and felt His breath
But I've wandered far from His side
And felt again the strains of death
Now I am running to find my Beloved
Longing His caresses again to feel
To know again His Holy kisses
To be in the very center of His will

Never again alone will I wander
For my place is to be at His side
For I've learned that the greatest honor
Is to be His heavenly Bride
Beloved I am drawing closer
Coming again to seek Your face
Longing to be held by Your caresses
Waiting to be kissed and in Your embrace

The Lord Is Leading Still!

Grateful I am
Of the Lord's leading still
And ever be grateful
I surely will

Thank you, Father
For holding my hand
And leading me on
To the Promised Land

~*~

The LORD is my shepherd; I shall not want.
He maketh me to lie down in green pastures:
He leadeth me beside the still waters. He
restoreth my soul: Psalm 23:1-3a

Abiding Courage

Oh for the courage to abide
Ever closer to His side
Humbly at Your feet, I pray
Lord, let me never go astray

And if by chance I should fall
And hear not Your loving call
Bring to mind Your scripture, sure
Reminding me but to endure

Show me the footprints in the sand
Where we have walked hand in hand
And of the times when things got rough
How that You then did pick me up

Carrying me, as we did go
Strengthening body, spirit and soul
Refreshing me against the tide
That I may evermore abide

~*~

Be of good courage, and He shall
strengthen your heart, all ye that hope in
the Lord. Psalm 31:24

BIBLE

The Bible is our <u>B</u>lueprint
To guide us through this life.
Written to <u>I</u>nstruct us
through temptation, pain and strife.
<u>B</u>elieving ALL it tells us
Will help us on the way
To <u>L</u>ive life as He intended it
<u>E</u>very single day!

BIBLE

<u>B</u>read of Life
<u>I</u>nspired <u>B</u>ook to feed the soul
<u>L</u>et's <u>E</u>at!

~*~

I don't know the author or origin of this
next anagram, but it fits our topic.

Basic

Instruction

Before

Leaving

Earth

All scripture is given by inspiration of
God, and is profitable for doctrine, for
reproof, for correction, for instruction in
righteousness: that the man of God may
be perfect, thoroughly furnished unto all
good works. 2 Timothy 3:16-17

God's Word Without Words

Walking through this world
Some men may never see
The Bible sitting on the table
Written for you and me.
And yet as we travel this upon old sod
There is an unwritten Word of God.
It is the Spirit of our Lord
Living within our hearts.
The smile we give to a child.
The Light we shine in the dark.
.Feeding of the poor or visiting the sick.
Or a soft word spoken, where anger would be quick.
We are only Bible that many folk will read
It is the small gestures of Jesus in you and me they see.

~*~

Ye are our epistle written on our hearts,
known and read of all men.
II Corinthians 3:2

Life And Death In Christ

Life as we know it is not really Life
Its struggling and weakness
It's combating stress and strife
It's pain and suffering and trying to cope
And sometimes we do find that small ray of hope
And if we keep on trying we learn the true story
That we bear it all better when we give God the glory

Death, much like life is not as we know
We're not really leaving, just going on with the flow
Behind we are leaving the pain of the past
True freedom to find from this body mortal at last
With Jesus our Lord and Savior eternity will be
Life with Him forever beyond the Crystal Sea

I know your afflictions and your poverty—yet you are rich! I know
the slander of those who say they are Jews and are not, but are a
synagogue of Satan. Do not be afraid of what you are about to suffer.
I tell you, the devil will put some of you in prison to test you, and you
will suffer persecution for ten days. Be faithful, even to the point of
death, and I will give you the crown of life. He who has an ear, let him
hear what the Spirit says to the churches. He who overcomes will not
be hurt at all
by the second death. Revelation 2:9-11

Journey's End

The end is set before us.
But the Way seems so unclear.
The Pathway winds through hill and dale
Yet climbs upwards every year.

Closer to the Master,
Growing more like Him each day.
Victorious o're all disaster,
As we battle through the fray.

Seeing but a few steps before us,
As He guides us gently on.
Giving Him all praises glorious,
As He gives to us the song.

Though the path seems dark before us,
We know He is our LIGHT within.
Protecting from what could be dangerous,
He safely brings us to journeys end.

~*~

For God so loved the world, that He gave
His only begotten Son, that whosoever
believeth on Him should not perish, but
have everlasting life. John 3:16

Journey's End

The Crown of Life

I seek not crowns of earthly fame
Nor wealth which bank vaults fill
I seek to glorify His name
And follow His holy will

I seek not worldly pleasures rare
Or notoriety
Instead I bow my head in prayer
And humble piety

The wealth I seek is not of gold
Or gems this world provides
It is to sit at Jesus' feet
And there with Him abide

For all the riches of this earth
Or the praise of men, renown
Do not compare to His gift of life
Or it's heavenly crown

~*~

Blessed is the man that endureth
temptation: for when he is tried, he shall
receive the crown of life, which the Lord
hath promised to them that love Him.
James 1:12

Crowned by The King

He has crowned me with the crown of Life,
That through His death I might live forever.
He has crowned me with the crown of
Righteousness; His, not mine. For my
righteousness is "as filthy rags" in His
presence.

He has crowned me with the crown of Peace.
His perfect Peace, which passes all understanding.
He has crowned me with the crown of true hope.
Hope of a life spent with Him throughout ALL eternity.

And all of these crowns I give back to Him. I humbly
lay them at His feet. The feet of the Prince of Peace,
King of Kings, And Lord of Lords in reverence for
ALL He has done for me! He is the soon and coming
King of ALL! My Lord, JESUS!

~*~

Henceforth there is laid up for me a crown of righteousness,
which the Lord, the righteous judge, shall give me at that day:
and not to me only, but unto all them also that love his
appearing. 2 Timothy 4:8

That Heavenly City

There in that city, that city so fair
There will be no worry, and nary a care
Only the light of God's perfect Love
Which now we view only in patches above

Follow me to Jesus as He lights the way
To that glorious city where joy never fades
Where peace abounds forever and life made is complete
As we bask in His glory forever sitting at His feet

~*~

And God shall wipe away all tears from
their eyes; and there shall be no more
death, neither sorrow, nor crying, neither
shall there be any more pain: for the
former things are passed away.
Revelation 21:4

What Are You Thinking?

What are you thinking, little one?
In your heart, what have you done?
What are you thinking little one; My little one?

Are there worries? Have you cares?
Are there heartaches anywhere?
What are you thinking little one; My little one?

Have you given Me your load?
I can turn your trials to gold
What are you thinking little one; My little one

In Me you will find rest
And such peace and happiness
When your thoughts are set on Me my little one.

In Honor of

Marriage,

Family

& Friends!

Marriage

Bands of Love

Bands of Silver, Bands of Gold
Symbols of our love they hold
Small and precious, round and hard
Totally perfect, like our Lord

When included in their life
God binds together man and wife
Walking together hands in Hand
United they journey to the promise land

Crowns of life from God are given
Gleaming bands of purest gold
When His bride meets Him in heaven
Their perfect union completed from days of old

And the glory which thou gavest me I have given them; that they may
be one, even as we are one: I in them, and thou in me, that they may
be made perfect in one; and that the world may know that thou hast
sent me, and hast loved them, as thou hast loved me. Father, I will
that they also, whom thou hast given me, be with me where I am; that
they may behold my glory, which thou hast given me: for thou lovedst
me before the foundation of the world. John 17:22-24

What God Has Joined

As God joins two people
Like He has both of you
It's a joyous occasion
That we celebrate, too

A joining of hearts
An entwining of souls
A wondrous music
As Love blooms and grows

Spread your music together
As you walk side by side
Bringing others to Jesus
As He is your guide

~*~

For this reason a man shall leave his father and mother and be joined
to his wife, and the two shall become one flesh. So then they are no
longer two, but one flesh. Therefore what God has joined together, let
not man separate. Matthew 19:5,6 NKJV

Two Become One

As you two become one
And your families combine
As your hearts intermingle
And your lives intertwine

May the Lord always bless you
And His Spirit always guide,
As you both grow together
And you work side by side

~*~

But from the beginning of the creation God made them male and female. For this cause shall a man leave his father and mother, and cleave to his wife; and they twain shall be one flesh: so then they are no more twain, but one flesh. What therefore God hath joined together, let not man put asunder. Mark 10:6-9

My Gifts To You

I gave my heart a gift to you when
Friendship did begin

I gave my heart again to you
As true love entered in

Renewed this gift again I gave
As each child started life

You are my Friend
My Love and My Beloved Wife

Each circle here does show
My gifts will never end

Forever I give all to you
My Wife, My Love, MY FRIEND!!!

~*~

God blessed me by allowing me to write and speak these words of love
from my Father to my Mother as a part of her Christmas gift in 2006.
He had a stroke years before and made it hard for him to express
himself in words.

I also had the privilege of doing his shopping that year as he was not
well. He gave me money and told me to pick up several nice pieces of
jewelry. I found five perfect pieces and the stanzas of the poem above
matched each one perfectly.

Only God, a giver of good gifts could have done such a wonderful job
of putting it all together. Thank you Lord! And thank You Lord, for
allowing me to share in their love and joy on this special occasion!

Family

Family

Families are Your gift to us, oh Lord. They show us, in a small way, an example of Your great love for us. Thank You for family. They are a safe harbor for us in times of trouble. We can lean on them in our weakness. Just as we can You in greater measure in any storm or battle that comes our way.

Amen.

~*~

In this same way, husbands ought to love their wives as their own bodies. He who loves his wife loves himself. After all, no one ever hated his own body, but he feeds and cares for it, just as Christ does the church— for we are members of his body. "For this reason a man will leave his father and mother and be united to his wife, and the two will become one flesh." This is a profound mystery—but I am talking about Christ and the church. However, each one of you also must love his wife as he loves himself, and the wife must respect her husband.

Ephesians 5:28-32

My Father

Truck driver, mechanic, builder of racecars
Provider and teacher; all of these you are

Builder of bodies and molder of souls
But all the while leaving God in control

Allowing us space to make some mistakes
Yet pointing us away from the ones that you made.

Asking forgiveness when God showed you how
You are my father; and I honor you now!

~*~

I Love You, Daddy!
Happy
Father's Day
2004

Mom and Pops

Happy Father's Day

F is for **F**aithful, **F**riendly and **F**ree

A **T** is for **A**lways being **T**here for we

H is for **H**ugging and **H**elping us through

Everyday struggles and pleasures, too

R is for the **R**adical turn of a phrase that
    helps us to grow with the passing of days

You may not be our father, but today we do.
Wish to Bless and Honor and Thank even you!

~*~

To all of the Fatherly examples God has
lovingly placed in each of our lives!

Two Little Angels

Two little Angels
Watching over you
One sits on your head
The other on your shoe

Though things may look bad
They tell me don't be blue
Our Heavenly Father
Is taking care of you

Some day, not so far off
We'll camp and pan for gold
By a mountain stream
Mom and Jimmy with us, too!

So just rest for now
With Angels one and two
And listen to all
The doctors are telling you to do

~*~

I Love You Pops!
6-14-2000

I wrote this for my father just after he had a stroke in 2000. I had bought a figurine of two angels to take to him while he was in the hospital. I gave him this poem with that small gift of love.

Father's Day Roundup

Roundin' up children
To celebrate their dad's
To let them know
All of the blessings we've had
The homes they've provided
The gifts that they gave
The lessons they've taught us
Our lives from sin to save

Roundin' up fathers
Our blessings to share
To let them all know
We will always care
Their roundin' up sinners
Their lost souls to save
To keep them from entering
Death, hell and the grave

And teaching them lessons
Of heaven above
And also of Jesus
Our Savior of Love
So that many will be gathered
When the last roundup is here
We'll all be laughing
And shouting a cheer

So roundup the fathers
And all ages of kids
Let the fathers speak of Jesus
Like these fathers did
To lead more kids to heaven
To Jesus Christ our King
To live with Him forever
And His praises to sing

Father's Day Roundup

Answering Our Mother's Prayers

Many are the times my foremothers
prayed for me. And God heard their
prayers, all of them. He has and is
answering them all, one by one. Just so, I
pray for my children and grandchildren.
For God to have His way in their lives.
For their happiness and their protection.
And I believe His promise to save my
'whole house." He will ultimately answer
this mother's prayers in His own way,
and by His own timetable.

~*~

My son (daughter), keep thy father's commandment, and forsake not
the law of thy mother: bind them continually upon thy heart and tie
them around your neck. When thou goest, it shall lead thee; and
when thou sleepest, it shall keep thee; and when thou awakest, it shall
talk with thee. Proverbs 6:20-22

Motherly Faith

In the dark of the night she sits silently by;
an old black Book in her lap and a tear in her eye.

She spent the night as so many before,
pouring her heart out unto the Lord

Praying salvation for those of her clan,
for every woman and every man.

For every child and all of her kin,
she's calling on Jesus to save them from sin.

She's heard all the lessons and learned every verse.
She knows what lies ahead; has prepared for the worst.

But still she sits praying for those she has raised. They've forsaken
Jesus; stopped singing His praise.

But her faith is grounded deep in his Word.
She has taken to heart every lesson she's heard.

And so she sits nightly her petitions to bring
to the feet of her Lord, our great King of kings!

And daily She trusts Him to answer her cry
and bring each into glory forever by and by.

~*~

Train up a child in the way he should go:
and when he is old, he will not depart from it.
Proverbs 22:6

The Lord's Mother's Day Gift

Lord, You gave us Mothers
To help us in the way
And so, again we honor them
On this, their special day

Help us, their load to lighten
As they journey on
And, too, their eyes to brighten
In word, or deed, or song

We love our Mothers dearly
And so we take this time
To honor them sincerely
Within this little rhyme

They picked us up and held us
As often we did fall
And helped us find those "missing things"
Whether book, or shoe, or doll

And so, we thank our Mothers
For leading us in part
Along life's winding journey
And to our Saviors heart

Thank You, God!
Happy Mother's Day
2005

Mother Of My Heart

Mothers are given from heaven above
And Mothers are chosen because of their love
You are the Mother that my heart has claimed
For you know all my dark times, and yet you remain

You're the one I seek for guidance when others leave me cold
You handle me with kindness, and yet you are so bold
God gave me you, my mother, when I was in need
I thank Him for His kindness, and for His gift, INDEED!

I Love You, Mom!

~*~

Special Day

Days may come
And Days may go
But Mother's Day
Is Special, you know
So I wanted to share
My Love with You
To let you know
That you're Special, too
And to let you know
That I love you!

Happy Mother's Day!
2010

The Family Tree

This Family Tree is bearer of ten fruits of jeweled stone
They portray you and those you call "your own"

Two daughters and three sons were the fruit of your womb
And four other daughters in your heart have found room

God gives us our family, while others we do choose
And these added daughters you did not want to loose

So they're added to your tree of love
Alongside those who share your blood

Grafted in branches, both new and old
Side by side with the natural and all dressed in pure gold

This family tree encircled with sweet, selfless love
It flows from all these precious fruit and is sent from above

So, wear this tree proudly, share its message with your friends
Thus insuring God's gifts of love to you will never end!

Happy Mother's Day 2010

~*~

This Mother's Day my brothers, sister, sisters-in-law and I bought our mother a Mother's Necklace to honor her on this special day. This poem was written and given to her for this special occasion.

We ALL Love You, MOM!

My Valentine's Prayer

This Valentine's Day my prayer shall be
A happy heart and home for thee
A smile to be upon your face
And your soul full with laughter and grace

Again your name to God I'll raise
And sing to Him my songs of praise
To tell Him of your friendship, dear
And how you let me bend your ear

May your heart with Son-shine be filled
As you endeavor to His Spirit to yield
I'll pray your pathway ever be clear
As always you strive His voice to hear

Lastly, I voice this prayer for you
That your heart may never be blue
And even if the sky looks gray
You'll know it won't always stay that way

~ Leigh ~
2-10-2009

Wonderful Brother

Wonderful brother, beautiful friend
Supporting his sister again and again
Driving for miles to fix an old car
Or repair a computer; he's my superstar

Staying up through the night
To make sure updates complete
Then stagers to the front room
While he's half asleep

This is my brother and very best friend
He has repeated these feats again and again
His valor is unknown to many a soul
But caring for his family is his highest goal

There are those who would 'dis' him
But they would be wrong
I would raise my voice often
To lift his praises in song

His name is David
But it's 'DJ' to me
He has the heart of a lion
And it's as big as the sea

Forever I will honor
My brother and my friend
For he has been faithful
To me again and again!

I Love you, Bro!
~ Leigh ~
07/08/2008

Wonderful Brother

This is D. J.
My Knight In Shining Armor!

Are All The Children In?

Are All The Children In? That may well be our question. But God already knows the answer. And He calms the fears of every mother's heart. He assures us that He will save our "whole house" and we cling to His promise, reminding Him time and again to draw our children in to His loving hands. He is ever faithful. Only Trust Him and continue to pray for their souls. Then ALL the Children will be in.

~*~

And brought them out, and said, Sirs, what must I do to be saved? And they said, Believe on the Lord Jesus Christ, and thou shalt be saved, and thy whole house. Acts 16: 30, 31

Lady Jady

Lady Jady, precious and sweet
Tend your gardens and keep them neat

Many flowers, both simple and rare
Can be found in your loving care

But flowering blooms will not long last
And gardening days, too, are soon past

So I've painted here this purple bloom
To always grace the walls of your room

Happy 90th Birthday
Gram

With all my love;
Leigh
1-24-2009

Grandma's Bible

It was sitting on the coffee table, Grandma's Bible, dusty and forgotten. Since she has moved into eternity no one has opened it's tattered pages to seek the wisdom and guidance within. Grandma always did. Daily you would find her sitting in her rocker early in the morning before anyone else was up and around.

Praying for her loved ones and pouring over it's pages. And in the dark hours of the night she'd be there again. Holding it like a cherished friend. In the solitude reading and rereading it's underlined passages.

And talk about LIGHT, her spirit was never in darkness. She was truly illuminated from within.
And she consistently walked out her life by it's whole counsel.

A few years ago I was feeling very depressed, full of darkness and gloom. So I picked up Grandma's Bible just by chance, or so I thought at the time. I let it fall open where it would – The Psalms. And I started reading. I couldn't –put it down.

Had the writer been in my room, hiding in my closet, listening to my cries? But I knew no one else had been there. And yet he felt my pain and heartache. Only he didn't stay in his darkness. So I continued to read. I
decided to follow his example. I found my way back into the Light, too.

I read more and more each day and found true hope and freedom in my spirit, Salvation in Jesus Christ. Now you can find me in Grandma's rocker before my day begins and again at the close of each day. Reading
my Bible and praying for the needs of my house.

I retired Grandma's Bible long ago. It was all but falling apart from it years of constant use, welcome friendship and never failing truth. It gives me the inner LIGHT she had all of her life. But I will carry the memories of her always in my heart, sitting in her rocker, meeting with Jesus on behalf of each of her family and friends daily. And one day I will be able to share with her the Legacy she left to me in the Bible she cherished in her heart and life when I see her again in Glory at Jesus feet.

This is but a story written in honor of my wonderful Grandma Jady; though many of its aspects are based in truth. She is a wonderful Christian woman and has been a blessing and inspiration to many others and myself. At this printing – summer 2010 – she is 91 years young and still as active as she can be both inside and outside of her home. I enjoy her company and she will be truly missed by a multitude of people when she joins eternity at the end of her earthly life.

Thank You Lord for this wonderful role model.
And thank you, Gram, for being their for me always!

~*~

Do not rebuke an older man harshly, but exhort him as if he were your father. Treat younger men as brothers, older women as mothers, and younger women as sisters, with absolute purity. Give proper recognition to those widows who are really in need.
1 Timothy 5:1-3. NIV.

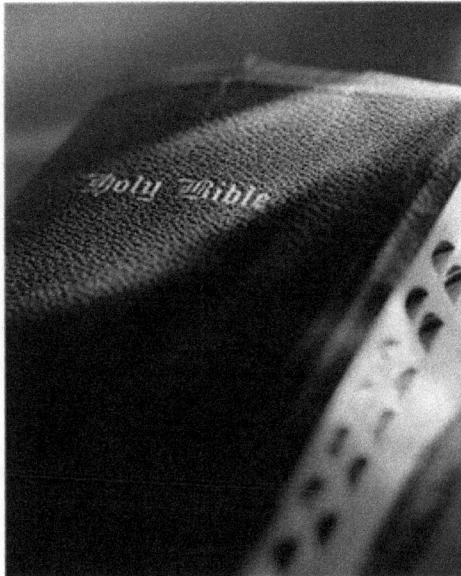

Appreciating Our Elders

The older I get Lord, the more I realize
that our elder saints are truly wise
beyond even their advancing years. They
have gained it from You. Throughout
their lives they have stored up the
memories of all You have done for them
and others of their loved ones. Many are
the miracles they have recorded. And
they can relate them to us when the need
arises. We should value and call upon
their wisdom. Thank You, Lord for the
gift of our elders.

~*~

The righteous shall flourish like the palm tree: he shall grow like a
cedar in Lebanon. Those that be planted in the house of the LORD
shall flourish in the courts of our God. They shall still bring forth
fruit in old age; they shall be fat and flourishing; To shew that the
LORD is upright: he is my rock, and there is no unrighteousness in
him. Psalm 92:12-15

Blessing Our Generations

Lord, thank You for blessing me with my
whole family. I have given them to You
time and time again. Today, I do so
again. Bring them close to Your heart
and hold them dear. That they will live
with You forever. My children and
grandchildren and so on right down
through the ages. Also my brothers,
sister, their spouses, children and
grandchildren, etc. That we may all live
in peace in Your Kingdom through all
eternity. Amen.

~*~

I pray for them: I pray not for the world, but for
them which thou hast given me; for they are thine.
John 17:9

Five Generations of my Family
From right: Papa Dick, Mom, Me & Brandi and Great Grandma
Clark

Five Generations of My Family
Behind: Mom [Nancy Morton]
Front: Me, Brandi Carroll, Grandma Jady Peters & Damon Sims

This Old House

**Mom's Family Home – ca 1950's
Sheridan, NY**

This Old House

This old house is not just a building
Made with walls and doors and glass
It is more than just a shelter
To protect from the storms that blast

This old house is a sanctuary
Fill with love, faith, peace and happiness
It is a hall filled with the memories
Of its long forgotten past

It's the joys of a new family
Starting life in wedded bliss
Holding hands and walking aimless
Of their first official kiss

It's the birth of their first child
Oh, how they waited so
And then the sorrow of his death
And of having to let go

It's the memories of the laughter
And of children running through the door
Of the joys and the sorrows
That they never knew before

Now their son's gone off to college
To study history and higher math
He has chosen academics
And looks toward his chosen path

The twins are just out of high school
And looking forward to their respective mates
And the double wedding
They are planning within these gates

There's a rose arbor in the garden
It will be the perfect place
Where the newly joined couples
Will greet their guests and celebrate

Mama and Papa have gone home to Jesus
And the children are grown and gone
The walls are all in need of paintin'
And overgrown with weeds is the lawn

But the house, it still remembers
All the laughter and the tears
All the joyous celebrations
And all the hidden fears

Now this house is old and empty
There's no laughter on the stair
How it creeks with the longing
Of the family who once lived there

But wait someone's coming
Holding hands, walking toward the door
Seems just like a memory
Has this happened once before?

There is a sweet, young couple
Peeking in through the window pane
They're whispering and they're planning
Oh, can it happen once again?

Can the walls be full to over flowing
With the peace and joy once known
Of a family just starting out together
And the love that is a growin'

The couple walk through the gardens
That were once mother's pride and joy
And discuss the thing they'd grow there
Hand of the hope of girls and boys

To share the love they have started
And this house that they did choose
To bless the neighborhood with laughter
And the patter of little shoes

Once again a sanctuary
Of a family and it's life
Once more the proud keeper
Of a man, his children and his wife

This old house was once forgotten
Yet now again it over flows
With the tears and with the joys
With the happiness and sorrows

Fulfilled for the purpose
For which his maker did create
When he first had the vision
And then hung the gate

And though this is a story
Of a house, it may be true
That it holds an example
Of life for me and you

For God created each one with a purpose
And it is still on His mind
Are you living as He intended
Or are you lagging behind?

~ Leigh ~
July 18, 2008

Traveler's Home

Welcome home weary travelers
We have longed for your return
We are glad you are home safely
For your stories we have yearned

We know God richly blessed you,
As you battled in L. A.
And now He'll surely rest you
As you're home for a stay

May His presence be increasing
As the Holy Spirit burns
A new flame in your lives daily
While you teach His truths you've learned

~*~

Written to honor the group sent from Honeyrock
(Christian Outreach Ministries)
Oroville, CA
To the Summer Olympics
Los Angeles, CA
July 1984

www.ingramcontent.com/pod-product-compliance
Lightning Source LLC
LaVergne TN
LVHW011348080426
835511LV00005B/191